A Raisin in the Sun

and Related Readings

McDougal Littell
A HOUGHTON MIFFLIN COMPANY

Evanston, Illinois   *Boston*   *Dallas*

Acknowledgments

Alfred A. Knopf, Inc.: "Dreams," from *The Dream Keeper and Other Poems* by Langston Hughes. Copyright 1932 by Alfred A. Knopf, Inc.; Copyright renewed © 1960 by Langston Hughes. Reprinted by permission of the publisher.

CALYX Books: "Emerald City: Third & Pike," from *Killing Color* by Charlotte Watson Sherman, published by CALYX Books, 1992.

Thunder's Mouth Press: "The Beach Umbrella," from *The Amoralists and Other Tales: Collected Stories b*y Cyrus Colter. Copyright © 1988 by Cyrus Colter. Used by permission of the publisher, Thunder's Mouth Press.

Susan Bergholz Literary Services: "Queens 1963," from *The Other Side/ El Otro Lado* by Julia Alvarez, 1995. Copyright © 1995 by Julia Alvarez. Published by Dutton, an imprint of Dutton Signet, a division of Penguin USA Inc. First published in *Patchwork of Dreams*.

Farrar, Straus & Giroux, Inc.: "Everything That Rises Must Converge," from *Everything That Rises Must Converge* by Flannery O'Connor. Copyright © 1965 by the Estate of Mary Flannery O'Connor. Copyright renewed © 1993 by Regina O'Connor. Reprinted by permission of Farrar, Straus & Giroux, Inc.

W. W. Norton & Company, Inc.: "Judith's Fancy," from *The Marvelous Arithmetics of Distance: Poems 1987–1992* by Audre Lorde. Copyright © 1993 by Audre Lorde. Reprinted with the permission of W. W. Norton & Company, Inc.

Money Magazine: "Running from Racists," by Suzanne Seixas, from the July 1991 issue of *Money*. Copyright © 1991, Time Inc. Reprinted by special permission of Money Magazine.

HarperCollins Publishers, Inc.: "What Is Africa to Me? A Question of Identity" pp. 328–332 from *Song in a Weary Throat: An American Pilgrimage* by Pauli Murray. Copyright © 1987 by The Estate of Pauli Murray. Reprinted by permission of HarperCollins Publishers, Inc. *A Raisin in the Sun* by Lorraine Hansberry, Copyright © 1958 by Robert Nemiroff, as an unpublished work. Copyright © 1959, 1966, 1984 by Robert Nemiroff. Reprinted by permission of Random House, Inc.

Cover illustration by Mark Braught.
Author photo: AP/Wide World Photos.
7—DCI—02 01 00

Contents

Continued

A Raisin in the Sun

Lorraine Hansberry

What happens to a dream deferred?
Does it dry up
Like a raisin in the sun?
Or fester like a sore—
And then run?
Does it stink like rotten meat?
Or crust and sugar over—
Like a syrupy sweet?

Maybe it just sags
Like a heavy load.

Or does it explode?

—Langston Hughes, "Harlem"

Cast of Characters

Ruth Younger

Travis Younger

Walter Lee Younger

Beneatha Younger

Lena Younger

Joseph Asagai

George Murchison

Karl Lindner

Bobo

Moving Men

Time: *Sometime between World War II and the present*

Place: *Chicago's South Side*

The Younger living room would be a comfortable and well-ordered room if it were not for a number of indestructible contradictions to this state of being. Its furnishings are typical and undistinguished, and their primary feature now is that they have clearly had to accommodate the living of too many people for too many years—and they are tired. Still, we can see that at some time, a time probably no longer remembered by the family (except perhaps for Mama), *the furnishings of this room were actually selected with care and love and even hope—and brought to this apartment and arranged with taste and pride.*

That was a long time ago. Now the once-loved pattern of the couch upholstery has to fight to show itself from under acres of crocheted doilies and couch covers that have themselves finally come to be more important than the upholstery. And here a table or a chair has been moved to disguise the worn places in the carpet; but the carpet has fought back by showing its weariness, with depressing uniformity, elsewhere on its surface.

Weariness has, in fact, won in this room. Everything has been polished, washed, sat on, used, scrubbed too often. All pretenses but living itself have long since vanished from the very atmosphere of this room.

Moreover, a section of this room, for it is not really a room unto itself, though the landlord's lease would make it seem so, slopes backward to provide a small kitchen area, where the family prepares the meals that are eaten in the living room proper, which must also serve as dining room. The single window that has been provided for these "two" rooms is located in this kitchen area. The sole natural light the family may enjoy in the course of a day is only that which fights its way through this little window.

At left, a door leads to a bedroom that is shared by Mama *and her daughter,* Beneatha. *At right, opposite, is a second room (which in the beginning of the life of this apartment was probably a breakfast room) that serves as a bedroom for* Walter *and his wife,* Ruth.

Act ONE

Scene 1 *Friday morning*

It is morning dark in the living room. Travis is asleep on the make-down bed at center. An alarm clock sounds from within the bedroom at right, and presently Ruth *enters from the room and closes the door behind her. She crosses sleepily toward the window. As she passes her sleeping son she reaches down and shakes him a little. At the window she raises the shade and a dusky South Side morning light comes in feebly. She fills a pot with water and puts it on to boil. She calls to the boy, between yawns, in a slightly muffled voice.*

Ruth *is about thirty. We can see that she was a pretty girl, even exceptionally so, but now it is apparent that life has been little that she expected, and disappointment has already begun to hang in her face. In a few years, before thirty-five even, she will be known among her people as a "settled woman."*

She crosses to her son and gives him a good, final, rousing shake.

Ruth. Come on now, boy, it's seven-thirty! (*Her son sits up at last, in a stupor of sleepiness.*) I say hurry up, Travis! You ain't the only person in the world got to use a bathroom! (*The child, a sturdy, handsome little boy of ten or eleven, drags himself out of the bed and almost blindly takes his towels and "today's clothes" from drawers and a closet and goes out to the bathroom, which is in an outside hall and which is shared by another* *family or families on the same floor.* Ruth *crosses to the bedroom door at right and opens it and calls in to her husband.*) Walter Lee! . . . It's after seven-thirty! Lemme see you do some waking up in there now! (*She waits.*) You better get up from there, man! It's after seven-thirty, I tell you. (*She waits again.*) All right, you just go ahead and lay there, and next thing you know Travis be finished and Mr. Johnson'll be in there and you'll be fussing and cussing round here like a mad man! And be late too! (*She waits, at the end of patience.*) Walter Lee— it's time for you to get up!

(*She waits another second and then starts to go into the bedroom but is apparently satisfied that her husband has begun to get up. She stops, pulls the door to, and returns to the kitchen area. She wipes her face with a moist cloth and runs her fingers through her sleep-disheveled hair in a vain effort and ties an apron around her housecoat. The bedroom door at right opens and her husband stands in the doorway in his pajamas, which are rumpled and mismated. He is a lean, intense young man in his middle thirties, inclined to quick nervous movements and erratic speech habits—and always in his voice there is a quality of indictment.*)

Walter. Is he out yet?

Ruth. What you mean *out*? He ain't hardly got in there good yet.

Walter (*wandering in, still more oriented to sleep than to a new day*). Well, what was you doing all that yelling for if I can't even get in there yet? (*stopping and thinking*) Check coming today?

Ruth. They *said* Saturday, and this is just Friday, and I hopes to God you ain't going to get up here first thing this morning and start talking to me 'bout no money—'cause I 'bout don't want to hear it.

Walter. Something the matter with you this morning?

Ruth. No—I'm just sleepy as the devil. What kind of eggs you want?

Walter. Not scrambled. (Ruth *starts to scramble eggs.*) Paper come? (Ruth *points impatiently to the rolled up* Tribune *on the table, and he gets it and spreads it out and vaguely reads the front page.*) Set off another bomb yesterday.

Ruth (*maximum indifference*). Did they?

Walter (*looking up*). What's the matter with you?

Ruth. Ain't nothing the matter with me. And don't keep asking me that this morning.

Walter. Ain't nobody bothering you. (*reading the news of the day absently again*) Say Colonel McCormick is sick.

Ruth (*affecting tea-party interest*). Is he now? Poor thing.

Walter (*sighing and looking at his watch*). Oh, me. (*He waits.*) Now what is that boy doing in that bathroom all this time? He just going to have to start getting up earlier. I can't be being late to work on account of him fooling around in there.

Ruth (*turning on him*). Oh, no, he ain't going to be getting up no earlier no such thing! It ain't his fault that he can't get to bed no earlier nights 'cause he got a bunch of crazy good-for-nothing clowns sitting up running their mouths in what is supposed to be his bedroom after ten o'clock at night . . .

Walter. That's what you mad about, ain't it? The things I want to talk about with my friends just couldn't be important in your mind, could they?

(*He rises and finds a cigarette in her handbag on the table* and crosses to the little window and looks out, smoking and deeply enjoying this first one.)

Ruth (*almost matter-of-factly, a complaint too automatic to deserve emphasis*). Why you always got to smoke before you eat in the morning?

Walter (*at the window*). Just look at 'em down there . . . Running and racing to work . . . (*He turns and faces his wife and watches her a moment at the stove, and then, suddenly.*) You look young this morning, baby.

Ruth (*indifferently*). Yeah?

Walter. Just for a second—stirring them eggs. It's gone now—just for a second it was—you looked real young again. (*then, drily*) It's gone now—you look like yourself again.

Ruth. Man, if you don't shut up and leave me alone.

Walter (*looking out to the street again*). First thing a man ought to learn in life is not to make love to no black woman first thing in the morning. You all some evil people at eight o'clock in the morning.

(Travis *appears in the hall doorway, almost fully dressed and quite wide awake now, his towels and pajamas across his shoulders. He opens the door and signals for his father to make the bathroom in a hurry.*)

Travis (*watching the bathroom*). Daddy, come on!

(Walter *gets his bathroom utensils and flies out to the bathroom.*)

Ruth. Sit down and have your breakfast, Travis.

Travis. Mama, this is Friday. (*gleefully*) Check coming tomorrow, huh?

Ruth. You get your mind off money and eat your breakfast.

Travis (*eating*). This is the morning we supposed to bring the fifty cents to school.

Ruth. Well, I ain't got no fifty cents this morning.

Travis. Teacher say we have to.

Ruth. I don't care what teacher say. I ain't got it. Eat your breakfast, Travis.

Travis. I *am* eating.

Ruth. Hush up now and just eat!

(*The boy gives her an exasperated look for her lack of understanding and eats grudgingly.*)

Travis. You think Grandmama would have it?

Ruth. No! And I want you to stop asking your grandmother for money, you hear me?

Travis (*outraged*). Gaaaleee! I don't ask her, she just gimme it sometimes!

Ruth. Travis Willard Younger—I got too much on me this morning to be—

Travis. Maybe Daddy—

Ruth. Travis!

(*The boy hushes abruptly. They are both quiet and tense for several seconds.*)

Travis (*presently*). Could I maybe go carry some groceries in front of the supermarket for a little while after school then?

Ruth. Just hush, I said. (Travis *jabs his spoon into his cereal bowl viciously and rests his head in anger upon his fists.*) If you through eating, you can get over there and make up your bed.

(*The boy obeys stiffly and crosses the room, almost me-chanically, to the bed and more or less carefully folds the covering. He carries the bedding into his mother's room and returns with his books and cap.*)

Travis (*sulking and standing apart from her unnaturally*). I'm gone.

Ruth (*looking up from the stove to inspect him auto-matically*). Come here. (*He crosses to her and she studies his head.*) If you don't take this comb and fix this here head, you better! (Travis *puts down his books with a great sigh of oppression, and crosses to the mirror. His mother mutters under her breath about his "slubborn-ness."*) 'Bout to march out of here with that head looking just like chickens slept in it! I just don't know where you get your slubborn ways . . . And get your jacket, too. Looks chilly out this morning.

Travis (*with conspicuously brushed hair and jacket*). I'm gone.

Ruth. Get carfare and milk money—(*waving one finger*)—and not a single penny for no caps, you hear me?

Travis (*with sullen politeness*). Yes'm.

(*He turns in outrage to leave. His mother watches after him as in his frustration he approaches the door almost comically. When she speaks to him, her voice has become a very gentle tease.*)

Ruth (*mocking; as she thinks he would say it*). Oh, Mama makes me so mad sometimes, I don't know what to do! (*She waits and continues to his back as he stands stock-still in front of the door.*) I wouldn't kiss that woman goodbye for nothing in this world this morning! (*The boy finally turns around and rolls his eyes at her, knowing the mood has changed and he is* *vindicated; he does not, however, move toward her yet.)* Not for nothing in this world! (*She finally laughs aloud at him and holds out her arms to him, and we see that it is a way between them, very old and practiced. He crosses to her and allows her to embrace him warmly but keeps his face fixed with masculine rigidity. She holds him back from her presently and looks at him and runs her fingers over the features of his face. With utter gentleness—)* Now— whose little old angry man are you?

Travis (*The masculinity and gruffness start to fade at last*). Aw gaalee—Mama. . . .

Ruth (*mimicking*). Aw—gaaaaalleeeee, Mama! (*She pushes him, with rough playfulness and finality, toward the door.*) Get on out of here or you going to be late.

Travis (*in the face of love, new aggressiveness*). Mama, could I *please* go carry groceries?

Ruth. Honey, it's starting to get so cold evenings.

Walter (*coming in from the bathroom and drawing a make-believe gun from a make-believe holster and shooting at his son*). What is it he wants to do?

Ruth. Go carry groceries after school at the super-market.

Walter. Well, let him go . . .

Travis (*quickly, to the ally*). I *have* to—she won't gimme the fifty cents . . .

Walter (*to his wife only*). Why not?

Ruth (*simply, and with flavor*). 'Cause we don't have it.

Walter (*to Ruth only*). What you tell the boy things like that for? (*reaching down into his pants with a rather important gesture*) Here, son—

(*He hands the boy the coin, but his eyes are directed to his wife's.* Travis *takes the money happily.*)

Travis. Thanks, Daddy.

(*He starts out.* Ruth *watches both of them with murder in her eyes.* Walter *stands and stares back at her with defiance, and suddenly reaches into his pocket again on an after-thought.*)

Walter (*without even looking at his son, still staring hard at his wife*). In fact, here's another fifty cents . . . Buy yourself some fruit today—or take a taxicab to school or something!

Travis. Whoopee—

(*He leaps up and clasps his father around the middle with his legs, and they face each other in mutual appreciation; slowly* Walter Lee *peeks around the boy to catch the violent rays from his wife's eyes and draws his head back as if shot.*)

Walter. You better get down now—and get to school, man.

Travis (*at the door*). OK. Goodbye.

(*He exits.*)

Walter (*after him, pointing with pride*). That's my boy. (*She looks at him in disgust and turns back to her work.*) You know what I was thinking 'bout in the bathroom this morning?

Ruth. No.

Walter. How come you always try to be so pleasant!

Ruth. What is there to be pleasant 'bout!

Walter. You want to know what I was thinking 'bout in the bathroom or not!

Ruth. I know what you thinking 'bout.

Walter (*ignoring her*). 'Bout what me and Willy Harris was talking about last night.

Ruth (*immediately—a refrain*). Willy Harris is a good-for-nothing loudmouth.

Walter. Anybody who talks to me has got to be a good-for-nothing loudmouth, ain't he? And what you know about who is just a good-for-nothing loudmouth? Charlie Atkins was just a "good-for-nothing loudmouth" too, wasn't he! When he wanted me to go in the dry-cleaning business with him. And now—he's grossing a hundred thousand a year. A hundred thousand dollars a year! You still call him a loudmouth!

Ruth (*bitterly*). Oh, Walter Lee. . . .

(*She folds her head on her arms over the table.*)

Walter (*rising and coming to her and standing over her*). You tired, ain't you? Tired of everything. Me, the boy, the way we live—this beat-up hole—everything. Ain't you? (*She doesn't look up, doesn't answer.*) So tired—moaning and groaning all the time, but you wouldn't do nothing to help, would you? You couldn't be on my side that long for nothing, could you?

Ruth. Walter, please leave me alone.

Walter. A man needs for a woman to back him up . . .

Ruth. Walter—

Walter. Mama would listen to you. You know she listen to you more than she do me and Bennie. She think more of you. All you have to do is just sit down with her when you drinking your coffee one morning and talking 'bout things like you do and—(*He sits down beside her and demonstrates* *graphically what he thinks her methods and tone should be.*)—you just sip your coffee, see, and say easy like that you been thinking 'bout that deal Walter Lee is so interested in, 'bout the store and all, and sip some more coffee, like what you saying ain't really that important to you—and the next thing you know, she be listening good and asking you questions, and when I come home—I can tell her the details. This ain't no fly-by-night proposition, baby. I mean we figured it out, me and Willy and Bobo.

Ruth (*with a frown*). Bobo?

Walter. Yeah. You see, this little liquor store we got in mind cost seventy-five thousand, and we figured the initial investment on the place be 'bout thirty thousand, see. That be ten thousand each. Course, there's a couple of hundred you got to pay so's you don't spend your life just waiting for them clowns to let your license get approved—

Ruth. You mean graft?

Walter (*frowning impatiently*). Don't call it that. See there, that just goes to show you what women understand about the world. Baby, don't *nothing* happen for you in this world 'less you pay *somebody* off!

Ruth. Walter, leave me alone! (*She raises her head and stares at him vigorously—then says, more quietly.*) Eat your eggs, they gonna be cold.

Walter (*straightening up from her and looking off*). That's it. There you are. Man say to his woman: I got me a dream. His woman say: Eat your eggs. (*sadly, but gaining in power*) Man say: I got to take hold of this here world, baby! And a woman will say: Eat your eggs and go to work. (*passionately now*) Man say: I got to change my life, I'm choking to death, baby! And his woman say—(*in utter anguish as he brings his fists down on his thighs*)—Your eggs is getting cold!

Ruth (*softly*). Walter, that ain't none of our money.

Walter (*not listening at all or even looking at her*). This morning, I was lookin' in the mirror and thinking about it . . . I'm thirty-five years old; I been married eleven years and I got a boy who sleeps in the living room—(*very, very quietly*)—and all I got to give him is stories about how rich white people live . . .

Ruth. Eat your eggs, Walter.

Walter. *Damn my eggs . . . damn all the eggs that ever was!*

Ruth. Then go to work.

Walter (*looking up at her*). See—I'm trying to talk to you 'bout myself—(*shaking his head with the repetition*)—and all you can say is eat them eggs and go to work.

Ruth (*wearily*). Honey, you never say nothing new. I listen to you every day, every night and every morning, and you never say nothing new. (*shrugging*) So you would rather *be* Mr. Arnold than be his chauffeur. So—I would *rather* be living in Buckingham Palace.

Walter. That is just what is wrong with the black woman in this world . . . Don't understand about building their men up and making 'em feel like they somebody. Like they can do something.

Ruth (*drily, but to hurt*). There *are* black men who do things.

Walter. No thanks to the black woman.

Ruth. Well, being a black woman, I guess I can't help myself none.

(*She rises and gets the ironing board and sets it up and attacks a huge pile of rough-dried clothes, sprinkling them in preparation for the ironing and then rolling them into tight fat balls.*)

Walter (*mumbling*). We one group of men tied to a race of women with small minds.

(*His sister Beneatha enters. She is about twenty, as slim and intense as her brother. She is not as pretty as her sister-in-law, but her lean, almost intellectual face has a handsomeness of its own. She wears a bright-red flannel nightie, and her thick hair stands wildly about her head. Her speech is a mixture of many things; it is different from the rest of the family's insofar as education has permeated her sense of English— and perhaps the Midwest rather than the South has finally—at last—won out in her inflection; but not altogether, because over all of it is a soft slurring and transformed use of vowels that is the decided influence of the South Side. She passes through the room without looking at either Ruth or Walter and goes to the outside door and looks, a little blindly, out to the bathroom. She sees that it has been lost to the Johnsons. She closes the door with a sleepy vengeance and crosses to the table and sits down a little defeated.*)

Beneatha. I am going to start timing those people.

Walter. You should get up earlier.

Beneatha (*Her face in her hands. She is still fighting the urge to go back to bed.*). Really—would you suggest dawn? Where's the paper?

Walter (*pushing the paper across the table to her as he studies her almost clinically, as though he has never seen her before*). You a horrible-looking chick at this hour.

Beneatha (*drily*). Good morning, everybody.

Walter (*senselessly*). How is school coming?

Beneatha (*in the same spirit*). Lovely. Lovely. And you know, biology is the greatest. (*looking up at him*) I dissected something that looked just like you yesterday.

Walter. I just wondered if you've made up your mind and everything.

Beneatha (*gaining in sharpness and impatience*). And what did I answer yesterday morning—and the day before that?

Ruth (*from the ironing board, like someone disinterested and old*). Don't be so nasty, Bennie.

Beneatha (*still to her brother*). And the day before that and the day before that!

Walter (*defensively*). I'm interested in you. Something wrong with that? Ain't many girls who decide—

Walter *and* **Beneatha** (*in unison*).—"to be a doctor." (*silence*)

Walter. Have we figured out yet just exactly how much medical school is going to cost?

Ruth. Walter Lee, why don't you leave that girl alone and get out of here to work?

Beneatha (*exits to the bathroom and bangs on the door*). Come on out of there, please!

(*She comes back into the room.*)

Walter (*looking at his sister intently*). You know the check is coming tomorrow.

Beneatha (*turning on him with a sharpness all her own*). That money belongs to Mama, Walter, and it's for her to decide how she wants to use it. I don't care if she wants to buy a house or a rocket ship or just nail it up somewhere and look at it. It's hers. Not ours—hers.

Walter (*bitterly*). Now ain't that fine! You just got your mother's interest at heart, ain't you, girl? You such a nice girl—but if Mama got that money she can always take a few thousand and help you through school too—can't she?

Beneatha. I have never asked anyone around here to do anything for me!

Walter. No! And the line between asking and just accepting when the time comes is big and wide—ain't it!

Beneatha (*with fury*). What do you want from me, Brother—that I quit school or just drop dead, which!

Walter. I don't want nothing but for you to stop acting holy 'round here. Me and Ruth done made some sacrifices for you—why can't you do something for the family?

Ruth. Walter, don't be dragging me in it.

Walter. You are in it—Don't you get up and go to work in somebody's kitchen for the last three years to help put clothes on her back?

Ruth. Oh, Walter—that's not fair . . .

Walter. It ain't that nobody expects you to get on your knees and say thank you, Brother; thank you, Ruth; thank you, Mama—and thank you, Travis, for wearing the same pair of shoes for two semesters—

Beneatha (*dropping to her knees*). Well—I *do*—all

right?—thank everybody . . . and forgive me for ever wanting to be anything at all . . . forgive me, forgive me!

Ruth. Please stop it! Your mama'll hear you.

Walter. Who the hell told you you had to be a doctor? If you so crazy 'bout messing 'round with sick people—then go be a nurse like other women—or just get married and be quiet . . .

Beneatha. Well—you finally got it said . . . It took you three years but you finally got it said. Walter, give up; leave me alone—it's Mama's money.

Walter. *He was my father, too!*

Beneatha. So what? He was mine, too—and Travis' grandfather—but the insurance money belongs to Mama. Picking on me is not going to make her give it to you to invest in any liquor stores— *(underbreath, dropping into a chair)*—and I for one say, God bless Mama for that!

Walter *(to Ruth).* See—did you hear? Did you hear!

Ruth. Honey, please go to work.

Walter. Nobody in this house is ever going to understand me.

Beneatha. Because you're a nut.

Walter. Who's a nut?

Beneatha. You—you are a nut. Thee is mad, boy.

Walter *(looking at his wife and his sister from the door, very sadly).* The world's most backward race of people, and that's a fact.

Beneatha *(turning slowly in her chair).* And then there are all those prophets who would lead us out of the wilderness—(Walter *slams out of the house.*)—into the swamps!

Ruth. Bennie, why you always gotta be pickin' on your brother? Can't you be a little sweeter sometimes? (*Door opens.* Walter *walks in.*)

Walter (*to* Ruth). I need some money for carfare.

Ruth (*looks at him, then warms; teasing, but tenderly*). Fifty cents? (*She goes to her bag and gets money.*) Here, take a taxi.

(Walter *exits.* Mama *enters. She is a woman in her early sixties, full-bodied and strong. She is one of those women of a certain grace and beauty who wear it so unobtrusively that it takes a while to notice. Her dark-brown face is surrounded by the total whiteness of her hair, and, being a woman who has adjusted to many things in life and overcome many more, her face is full of strength. She has, we can see, wit and faith of a kind that keep her eyes lit and full of interest and expectancy. She is, in a word, a beautiful woman. Her bearing is perhaps most like the noble bearing of the women of the Hereros of Southwest Africa—rather as if she imagines that as she walks she still bears a basket or a vessel upon her head. Her speech, on the other hand, is as careless as her carriage is precise—she is inclined to slur everything— but her voice is perhaps not so much quiet as simply soft.*)

Mama. Who that 'round here slamming doors at this hour?

(*She crosses through the room, goes to the window, opens it, and brings in a feeble little plant growing doggedly in a small pot on the window sill. She feels the dirt and puts it back out.*)

Ruth. That was Walter Lee. He and Bennie was at it again.

Mama. My children and they tempers. Lord, if this

little old plant don't get more sun than it's been getting it ain't never going to see spring again. (*She turns from the window.*) What's the matter with you this morning, Ruth? You looks right peaked. You aiming to iron all them things? Leave some for me. I'll get to 'em this afternoon. Bennie honey, it's too drafty for you to be sitting 'round half dressed. Where's your robe?

Beneatha. In the cleaners.

Mama. Well, go get mine and put it on.

Beneatha. I'm not cold, Mama, honest.

Mama. I know—but you so thin . . .

Beneatha (*irritably*). Mama, I'm not cold.

Mama (*seeing the make-down bed as* Travis *has left it*). Lord have mercy, look at that poor bed. Bless his heart—he tries, don't he?

(*She moves to the bed* Travis *has sloppily made up.*)

Ruth. No—he don't half try at all 'cause he knows you going to come along behind him and fix everything. That's just how come he don't know how to do nothing right now—you done spoiled that boy so.

Mama. Well—he's a little boy. Ain't supposed to know 'bout housekeeping. My baby, that's what he is. What you fix for his breakfast this morning?

Ruth (*angrily*). I feed my son, Lena!

Mama. I ain't meddling—(*underbreath; busy-bodyish*) I just noticed all last week he had cold cereal, and when it starts getting this chilly in the fall a child ought to have some hot grits or something when he goes out in the cold—

Ruth (*furious*). I gave him hot oats—is that all right!

Mama. I ain't meddling. (*pause*) Put a lot of nice butter on it? (Ruth *shoots her an angry look and does not reply.*) He likes lots of butter.

Ruth (*exasperated*). Lena—

Mama (*To* Beneatha. Mama *is inclined to wander conversationally sometimes*). What was you and your brother fussing 'bout this morning?

Beneatha. It's not important, Mama.

(*She gets up and goes to look out at the bathroom, which is apparently free, and she picks up her towels and rushes out.*)

Mama. What was they fighting about?

Ruth. Now you know as well as I do.

Mama (*shaking her head*). Brother still worrying hisself sick about that money?

Ruth. You know he is.

Mama. You had breakfast?

Ruth. Some coffee.

Mama. Girl, you better start eating and looking after yourself better. You almost thin as Travis.

Ruth. Lena—

Mama. Un-hunh?

Ruth. What are you going to do with it?

Mama. Now don't you start, child. It's too early in the morning to be talking about money. It ain't Christian.

Ruth. It's just that he got his heart set on that store—

Mama. You mean that liquor store that Willy Harris wants him to invest in?

Ruth. Yes—

Mama. We ain't no business people, Ruth. We just plain working folks.

Ruth. Ain't nobody business people till they go into business. Walter Lee say black people ain't never going to start getting ahead till they start gambling on some different kinds of things in the world— investments and things.

Mama. What done got into you, girl? Walter Lee done finally sold you on investing.

Ruth. No. Mama, something is happening between Walter and me. I don't know what it is—but he needs something—something I can't give him any more. He needs this chance, Lena.

Mama (*frowning deeply*). But liquor, honey—

Ruth. Well—like Walter say—I spec people going to always be drinking themselves some liquor.

Mama. Well—whether they drinks it or not ain't none of my business. But whether I go into business selling it to 'em *is*, and I don't want that on my ledger this late in life. (*stopping suddenly and studying her daughter-in-law*) Ruth Younger, what's the matter with you today? You look like you could fall over right there.

Ruth. I'm tired.

Mama. Then you better stay home from work today.

Ruth. I can't stay home. She'd be calling up the agency and screaming at them, "My girl didn't come in today—send me somebody! My girl didn't come in!" Oh, she just have a fit . . .

Mama. Well, let her have it. I'll just call her up and say you got the flu—

Ruth (*laughing*). Why the flu?

Mama. 'Cause it sounds respectable to 'em. Something white people get, too. They know 'bout the flu. Otherwise they think you been cut up or something when you tell 'em you sick.

Ruth. I got to go in. We need the money.

Mama. Somebody would of thought my children done all but starved to death the way they talk about money here late. Child, we got a great big old check coming tomorrow.

Ruth (*sincerely, but also self-righteously*). Now that's your money. It ain't got nothing to do with me. We all feel like that—Walter and Bennie and me—even Travis.

Mama (*thoughtfully, and suddenly very far away*). Ten thousand dollars—

Ruth. Sure is wonderful.

Mama. Ten thousand dollars.

Ruth. You know what you should do, Miss Lena? You should take yourself a trip somewhere. To Europe or South America or someplace—

Mama (*throwing up her hands at the thought*). Oh, child!

Ruth. I'm serious. Just pack up and leave! Go on away and enjoy yourself some. Forget about the family and have yourself a ball for once in your life—

Mama (*drily*). You sound like I'm just about ready to die. Who'd go with me? What I look like wandering 'round Europe by myself?

Ruth. Shoot—these here rich white women do it all the time. They don't think nothing of packing up they suitcases and piling on one of them big steamships and—swoosh!—they gone, child.

Mama. Something always told me I wasn't no rich white woman.

Ruth. Well—what are you going to do with it then?

Mama. I ain't rightly decided. (*Thinking. She speaks now with emphasis.*) Some of it got to be put away for Beneatha and her schoolin'—and ain't nothing going to touch that part of it. Nothing. (*She waits several seconds, trying to make up her mind about something, and looks at* Ruth *a little tentatively before going on.*) Been thinking that we maybe could meet the notes on a little old two-story somewhere, with a yard where Travis could play in the summertime, if we use part of the insurance for a down payment and everybody kind of pitch in. I could maybe take on a little day work again, few days a week—

Ruth (*studying her mother-in-law furtively and concentrating on her ironing, anxious to encourage without seeming to*). Well, Lord knows, we've put enough rent into this here rat trap to pay for four houses by now . . .

Mama (*looking up at the words "rat trap" and then looking around and leaning back and sighing—in a suddenly reflective mood*). "Rat trap"—yes, that's all it is. (*smiling*) I remember just as well the day me and Big Walter moved in here. Hadn't been married but two weeks and wasn't planning on living here no more than a year. (*She shakes her head at the dissolved dream.*) We was going to set away, little by little, don't you know, and buy a little place out in Morgan Park. We had even picked out the house. (*chuckling a little*) Looks right dumpy today. But Lord, child, you should know all the dreams I had 'bout buying that house and fixing it up and making me a little garden in the back—(*She waits and stops smiling.*) And didn't none of it happen. (*dropping her hands in a futile gesture*)

Ruth (*keeps her head down, ironing*). Yes, life can be a barrel of disappointments, sometimes.

Mama. Honey, Big Walter would come in here some nights back then and slump down on that couch there and just look at the rug, and look at me and look at the rug and then back at me—and I'd know he was down then . . . really down. (*After a second very long and thoughtful pause; she is seeing back to times that only she can see.*) And then, Lord, when I lost that baby—little Claude—I almost thought I was going to lose Big Walter too. Oh, that man grieved hisself! He was one man to love his children.

Ruth. Ain't nothin' can tear at you like losin' your baby.

Mama. I guess that's how come that man finally worked hisself to death like he done. Like he was fighting his own war with this here world that took his baby from him.

Ruth. He sure was a fine man, all right. I always liked Mr. Younger.

Mama. Crazy 'bout his children! God knows there was plenty wrong with Walter Younger—hard-headed, mean, kind of wild with women—plenty wrong with him. But he sure loved his children. Always wanted them to have something—be something. That's where Brother gets all these notions, I reckon. Big Walter used to say, he'd get right wet in the eyes sometimes, lean his head back with the water standing in his eyes and say, "Seem like God didn't see fit to give the black man nothing but dreams—but He did give us children to make them dreams seem worthwhile." (*She smiles.*) He could talk like that, don't you know.

Ruth. Yes, he sure could. He was a good man, Mr. Younger.

Mama. Yes, a fine man—just couldn't never catch up with his dreams, that's all.

(Beneatha *comes in, brushing her hair and looking up to the ceiling, where the sound of a vacuum cleaner has started up.*)

Beneatha. What could be so dirty on that woman's rugs that she has to vacuum them every single day?

Ruth. I wish certain young women 'round here who I could name would take inspiration about certain rugs in a certain apartment I could also mention.

Beneatha (*shrugging*). How much cleaning can a house need?

Mama. Bennie!

Ruth. Just listen to her—just listen!

Beneatha. Oh, God!

Mama. If you use the Lord's name just one more time—

Beneatha (*a bit of whine*). Oh, Mama—

Ruth. Fresh—just fresh as salt, this girl!

Beneatha (*drily*). Well—if the salt loses its savor—

Mama. Now that will do. I just ain't going to have you 'round here reciting the scriptures in vain—you hear me?

Beneatha. How did I manage to get on everybody's wrong side by just walking into a room?

Ruth. If you weren't so fresh—

Beneatha. Ruth, I'm twenty years old.

Mama. What time you be home from school today?

Beneatha. Kind of late. (*with enthusiasm*) Madeline is going to start my guitar lessons today.

(Mama *and* Ruth *look up with the same expression.*)

Mama. Your *what* kind of lessons?

Beneatha. Guitar.

Ruth. Oh, Father!

Mama. How come you done taken it in your mind to learn to play the guitar?

Beneatha. I just want to, that's all.

Mama (*smiling*). Lord, child, don't you know what to do with yourself? How long it going to be before you get tired of this now—like you got tired of that little play-acting group you joined last year? (*looking at* Ruth) And what was it the year before that?

Ruth. The horseback-riding club for which she bought that fifty-five-dollar riding habit that's been hanging in the closet ever since!

Mama (*to* Beneatha). Why you got to flit so from one thing to another, baby?

Beneatha (*sharply*). I just want to learn to play the guitar. Is there anything wrong with that?

Mama. Ain't nobody trying to stop you. I just wonders sometimes why you has to flit so from one thing to another all the time. You ain't never done nothing with all that camera equipment you brought home—

Beneatha. I don't flit! I—I experiment with different forms of expression—

Ruth. Like riding a horse?

Beneatha. People have to express themselves one way or another.

Mama. What is it you want to express?

Beneatha (*angrily*). Me! (Mama *and* Ruth *look at each other and burst into raucous laughter.*) Don't worry—I don't expect you to understand.

Mama (*to change the subject*). Who you going out with tomorrow night?

Beneatha (*with displeasure*). George Murchison again.

Mama (*pleased*). Oh—you getting a little sweet on him?

Ruth. You ask me, this child ain't sweet on nobody but herself—(*underbreath*) Express herself!

(*They laugh.*)

Beneatha. Oh—I like George all right, Mama. I mean I like him enough to go out with him and stuff, but—

Ruth (*for devilment*). What does *and stuff* mean?

Beneatha. Mind your own business.

Mama. Stop picking at her now, Ruth. (*a thoughtful pause, and then a suspicious sudden look at her daughter as she turns in her chair for emphasis*) What *does* it mean?

Beneatha (*wearily*). Oh, I just mean I couldn't ever really be serious about George. He's—he's so shallow.

Ruth. Shallow—what do you mean he's shallow? He's *Rich!*

Mama. Hush, Ruth.

Beneatha. I know he's rich. He knows he's rich, too.

Ruth. Well—what other qualities a man got to have to satisfy you, little girl?

Beneatha. You wouldn't even begin to understand. Anybody who married Walter could not possibly understand.

Mama (*outraged*). What kind of way is that to talk about your brother?

Beneatha. Brother is a flip—let's face it.

Mama (*to* Ruth, *helplessly*). What's a flip?

Ruth (*glad to add kindling*). She's saying he's crazy.

Beneatha. Not crazy. Brother isn't really crazy yet—he—he's an elaborate neurotic.

Mama. Hush your mouth!

Beneatha. As for George. Well. George looks good—he's got a beautiful car and he takes me to nice places and, as my sister-in-law says, he is probably the richest boy I will ever get to know and I even like him sometimes—but if the Youngers are sitting around waiting to see if their little Bennie is going to tie up the family with the Murchisons, they are wasting their time.

Ruth. You mean you wouldn't marry George Murchison if he asked you someday? That pretty, rich thing? Honey, I knew you was odd—

Beneatha. No I would not marry him if all I felt for him was what I feel now. Besides, George's family wouldn't really like it.

Mama. Why not?

Beneatha. Oh, Mama—The Murchisons are honest-to-God-real-*live*-rich black people, and the only people in the world who are more snobbish than rich white people are rich black people. I thought everybody knew that. I've met Mrs. Murchison. She's a scene!

Mama. You must not dislike people 'cause they well off, honey.

Beneatha. Why not? It makes just as much sense as disliking people 'cause they are poor, and lots of people do that.

Ruth (*A wisdom-of-the-ages manner. To* Mama). Well, she'll get over some of this—

Beneatha. Get over it? What are you talking about, Ruth? Listen, I'm going to be a doctor. I'm not worried about who I'm going to marry yet—if I ever get married.

Mama *and* **Ruth.** *If!*

Mama. Now, Bennie—

Beneatha. Oh, I probably will . . . but first I'm going to be a doctor, and George, for one, still thinks that's pretty funny. I couldn't be bothered with that. I am going to be a doctor, and everybody around here better understand that!

Mama (*kindly*). 'Course you going to be a doctor, honey, God willing.

Beneatha (*drily*). God hasn't got a thing to do with it.

Mama. Beneatha—that just wasn't necessary.

Beneatha. Well—neither is God. I get sick of hearing about God.

Mama. Beneatha!

Beneatha. I mean it! I'm just tired of hearing about God all the time. What has He got to do with anything? Does he pay tuition?

Mama. You 'bout to get your fresh little jaw slapped!

Ruth. That's just what she needs, all right!

Beneatha. Why? Why can't I say what I want to around here, like everybody else?

Mama. It don't sound nice for a young girl to say things like that—you wasn't brought up that way. Me and your father went to trouble to get you and Brother to church every Sunday.

Beneatha. Mama, you don't understand. It's all a matter of ideas, and God is just one idea I don't accept. It's not important. I am not going out and be immoral or commit crimes because I don't believe in God. I don't even think about it. It's just that I get tired of Him getting credit for all the things the human race achieves through its own stubborn effort. There simply is no God—there is only man and it is he who makes miracles!

(Mama *absorbs this speech, studies her daughter and rises slowly and crosses to* Beneatha *and slaps her powerfully across the face. After, there is only silence and the daughter drops her eyes from her mother's face, and* Mama *is very tall before her.*)

Mama. Now—you say after me, in my mother's house there is still God. (*There is a long pause and* Beneatha *stares at the floor wordlessly.* Mama *repeats the phrase with precision and cool emotion.*) In my mother's house there is still God.

Beneatha. In my mother's house there is still God.

(a long pause)

Mama (Walking away from Beneatha, too disturbed for triumphant posture. Stopping and turning back to her daughter.). There are some ideas we ain't going to have in this house. Not long as I am at the head of this family.

Beneatha. Yes, ma'am.

(Mama walks out of the room.)

Ruth (almost gently, with profound understanding). You think you a woman, Bennie—but you still a little girl. What you did was childish—so you got treated like a child.

Beneatha. I see. (quietly) I also see that everybody thinks it's all right for Mama to be a tyrant. But all the tyranny in the world will never put a God in the heavens!

(She picks up her books and goes out.)

Ruth (goes to Mama's door). She said she was sorry.

Mama (coming out, going to her plant). They frightens me, Ruth. My children.

Ruth. You got good children, Lena. They just a little off sometimes—but they're good.

Mama. No—there's something come down between me and them that don't let us understand each other, and I don't know what it is. One done almost lost his mind thinking 'bout money all the time, and the other done commence to talk about things I can't seem to understand in no form or fashion. What is it that's changing, Ruth?

Ruth (*soothingly, older than her years*). Now . . . you taking it all too seriously. You just got strong-willed children and it takes a strong woman like you to keep 'em in hand.

Mama (*looking at her plant and sprinkling a little water on it*). They spirited all right, my children. Got to admit they got spirit—Bennie and Walter. Like this little old plant that ain't never had enough sunshine or nothing—and look at it . . .

(*She has her back to* Ruth, *who has had to stop ironing and lean against something and put the back of her hand to her forehead.*)

Ruth (*trying to keep* Mama *from noticing*). You . . . sure . . . loves that little old thing, don't you? . . .

Mama. Well, I always wanted me a garden like I used to see sometimes at the back of the houses down home. This plant is close as I ever got to having one. (*She looks out of the window as she replaces the plant.*) Lord, ain't nothing as dreary as the view from this window on a dreary day, is there? Why ain't you singing this morning, Ruth? Sing that "No Ways Tired." That song always lifts me up so—(*She turns at last to see that* Ruth *has slipped quietly into a chair, in a state of semiconsciousness.*) Ruth! Ruth honey—what's the matter with you . . . Ruth!

Scene 2

It is the following morning, a Saturday morning, and house cleaning is in progress at the Youngers. Furniture has been shoved hither and yon, and Mama *is giving the kitchen-area walls a washing down.* Beneatha, *in dungarees, with a handkerchief tied around her face, is spraying insecticide into the cracks in the walls. As they work, the radio is on and a South Side disk-jockey program is inappropriately filling the house with a rather exotic saxophone blues.* Travis, *the sole idle one, is leaning on his arms, looking out of the window.*

Travis. Grandmama, that stuff Bennie is using smells awful. Can I go downstairs, please?

Mama. Did you get all them chores done already? I ain't seen you doing much.

Travis. Yes'm—finished early. Where did Mama go this morning?

Mama (*looking at* Beneatha). She had to go on a little errand.

Travis. Where?

Mama. To tend to her business.

Travis. Can I go outside then?

Mama. Oh, I guess so. You better stay right in front of the house, though . . . and keep a good lookout for the postman.

Travis. Yes'm. (*He starts out and decides to give his* Aunt Beneatha *a good swat on the legs as he passes her.*) Leave them poor little old cockroaches alone, they ain't bothering you none.

(*He runs as she swings the spray gun at him both viciously and playfully.* Walter *enters from the bedroom and goes to the phone.*)

Mama. Look out there, girl, before you be spilling some of that stuff on that child!

Travis (*teasing*). That's right—look out now!

(*He exits.*)

Beneatha (*drily*). I can't imagine that it would hurt him—it has never hurt the roaches.

Mama. Well, little boys' hides ain't as tough as South Side roaches.

Walter (*into phone*). Hello—Let me talk to Willy Harris.

Mama. You better get over there behind the bureau. I seen one marching out of there like Napoleon yesterday.

Walter. Hello, Willy? It ain't come yet. It'll be here in a few minutes. Did the lawyer give you the papers?

Beneatha. There's really only one way to get rid of them, Mama—

Mama. How?

Beneatha. Set fire to this building.

Walter. Good. Good. I'll be right over.

Beneatha. Where did Ruth go, Walter?

Walter. I don't know.

(*He exits abruptly.*)

Beneatha. Mama, where did Ruth go?

Mama (*looking at her with meaning*). To the doctor, I think.

Beneatha. The doctor? What's the matter? (*They exchange glances.*) You don't think—

Mama (*with her sense of drama*). Now I ain't saying what I think. But I ain't never been wrong 'bout a woman neither.

(*The phone rings.*)

Beneatha (*at the phone*). Hay-lo. . . . (*pause, and a moment of recognition*) Well—when did you get back! . . . And how was it? . . . Of course I've missed you—in my way . . . This morning? No . . . house cleaning and all that and Mama hates it if I let people come over when the house is like this . . . You *have?* Well, that's different . . . What is it—Oh, what the heck, come on over . . . Right, see you then.

(*She hangs up.*)

Mama (*who has listened vigorously, as is her habit*). Who is that you inviting over here with this house looking like this? You ain't got the pride you was born with!

Beneatha. Asagai doesn't care how houses look, Mama—he's an intellectual.

Mama. *Who?*

Beneatha. Asagai—Joseph Asagai. He's an African boy I met on campus. He's been studying in Canada all summer.

Mama. What's his name?

Beneatha. Asagai, Joseph. As-sah-guy . . . He's from Nigeria.

Mama. Oh, that's the little country that was founded by slaves way back . . .

Beneatha. No, Mama—that's Liberia.

Mama. I don't think I never met no African before.

Beneatha. Well, do me a favor and don't ask him a whole lot of ignorant questions about Africans. I mean, do they wear clothes and all that—

Mama. Well, now, I guess if you think we so ignorant 'round here maybe you shouldn't bring your friends here—

Beneatha. It's just that people ask such crazy things. All anyone seems to know about when it comes to Africa is Tarzan—

Mama (*indignantly*). Why should I know anything about Africa?

Beneatha. Why do you give money at church for the missionary work?

Mama. Well, that's to help save people.

Beneatha. You mean save them from *heathenism*—

Mama (*innocently*). Yes.

Beneatha. I'm afraid they need more salvation from the British and the French.

(Ruth *comes in forlornly and pulls off her coat with dejection. They both turn to look at her.*)

Ruth (*dispiritedly*). Well, I guess from all the happy faces—everybody knows.

Beneatha. You pregnant?

Mama. Lord have mercy, I sure hope it's a little old girl. Travis ought to have a sister.

(Beneatha *and* Ruth *give her a hopeless look for this grand-motherly enthusiasm.*)

Beneatha. How far along are you?

Ruth. Two months.

Beneatha. Did you mean to? I mean did you plan it or was it an accident?

Mama. What do you know about planning or not planning?

Beneatha. Oh, Mama.

Ruth (*wearily*). She's twenty years old, Lena.

Beneatha. Did you plan it, Ruth?

Ruth. Mind your own business.

Beneatha. It is my business—where is he going to live, on the roof? (*There is silence following the remark as the three women react to the sense of it.*) Gee—I didn't mean that, Ruth, honest. Gee, I don't feel like that at all. I—I think it is wonderful.

Ruth (*dully*). Wonderful.

Beneatha. Yes—really.

Mama (*looking at* Ruth, *worried*). Doctor say everything going to be all right?

Ruth (*far away*). Yes—she says everything is going to be fine . . .

Mama (*immediately suspicious*). "She"—What doctor you went to?

(Ruth *folds over, near hysteria.*)

Mama (*worriedly hovering over* Ruth). Ruth honey—what's the matter with you—you sick?

(Ruth *has her fists clenched on her thighs and is fighting hard to suppress a scream that seems to be rising in her.*)

Beneatha. What's the matter with her, Mama?

Mama (*working her fingers in* Ruth's *shoulder to relax her*). She be all right. Women gets right depressed sometimes when they get her way. (*speaking softly, expertly, rapidly*) Now you just relax. That's right . . . just lean back, don't think 'bout nothing at all . . . nothing at all—

Ruth. I'm all right . . .

(*The glassy-eyed look melts and then she collapses into a fit of heavy sobbing. The bell rings.*)

Beneatha. Oh—that must be Asagai.

Mama (*to* Ruth). Come on now, honey. You need to lie down and rest awhile . . . then have some nice hot food.

(*They exit,* Ruth's *weight on her mother-in-law.* Beneatha, *herself profoundly disturbed, opens the door to admit a rather dramatic-looking young man with a large package.*)

Asagai. Hello, Alaiyo—

Beneatha (*holding the door open and regarding him with pleasure*). Hello . . . (*long pause*) Well—come in. And please excuse everything. My mother was very upset about my letting anyone come here with the place like this.

Asagai (*coming into the room*). You look disturbed too . . . Is something wrong?

Beneatha (*still at the door, absently*). Yes . . . we've all got acute ghetto-itus (*She smiles and comes toward him, finding a cigarette and sitting.*) So—sit down! How was Canada?

Asagai (*a sophisticate*). Canadian.

Beneatha (*looking at him*). I'm very glad you are back.

Asagai (*looking back at her in turn*). Are you really?

Beneatha. Yes—very.

Asagai. Why—you were quite glad when I went away. What happened?

Beneatha. You went away.

Asagai. Ahhhhhhhh.

Beneatha. Before—you wanted to be so serious before there was time.

Asagai. How much time must there be before one knows what one feels?

Beneatha (*Stalling this particular conversation. Her hands pressed together, in a deliberately childish gesture.*). What did you bring me?

Asagai (*handing her the package*). Open it and see.

Beneatha (*eagerly opening the package and drawing out some records and the colorful robes of a Nigerian woman*). Oh, Asagai! . . . You got them for me! . . . How beautiful . . . and the records too! (*She lifts out the robes and runs to the mirror with them and holds the drapery up in front of herself.*)

Asagai (*coming to her at the mirror*). I shall have to teach you how to drape it properly. (*He flings the material about her for the moment and stands back to look at her.*) Ah—*Oh-pay-gay-day, oh-gbah-mu-shay* [*a Yoruba exclamation for admiration*]. You wear it well . . . very well . . . mutilated hair and all.

Beneatha (*turning suddenly*). My hair—what's wrong with my hair?

Asagai (*shrugging*). Were you born with it like that?

Beneatha (*reaching up to touch it*). No . . . of course not.

(*She looks back to the mirror, disturbed.*)

Asagai (*smiling*). How then?

Beneatha. You know perfectly well how . . . as crinkly as yours . . . that's how.

Asagai. And it is ugly to you that way?

Beneatha (*quickly*). Oh, no—not ugly . . . (*more slowly, apologetically*) But it's so hard to manage when it's, well—raw.

Asagai. And so to accommodate that—you mutilate it every week?

Beneatha. It's not mutilation!

Asagai (*laughing aloud at her seriousness*). Oh . . . please! I am only teasing you because you are so very serious about these things. (*He stands back from her and folds his arms across his chest as he watches her pulling at her hair and frowning in the mirror.*) Do you remember the first time you met me at school? . . . (*He laughs.*) You came up to me and you said—and I thought you were the most serious little thing I had ever seen—you said: (*He imitates her.*) "Mr. Asagai— I want very much to talk with you. About Africa. You see, Mr. Asagai, I am looking for my *identity!*"

(*He laughs.*)

Beneatha (*turning to him, not laughing*). Yes—

(*Her face is quizzical, profoundly disturbed.*)

Asagai (*still teasing and reaching out and taking her face in his hands and turning her profile to him*). Well . . . it is true that this is not so much a profile of a Hollywood queen as perhaps a queen of the Nile—(*a mock dismissal of the importance of the question*) But what does it matter? Assimilationism is so popular in your country.

Beneatha (*wheeling, passionately, sharply*). I am not an assimilationist!

Asagai (*The protest hangs in the room for a moment and Asagai studies her, his laughter fading.*). Such a serious one. (*There is a pause.*) So—you like the robes? You must take excellent care of them—they are from my sister's personal wardrobe.

Beneatha (*with incredulity*). You—you sent all the way home—for me?

Asagai (*with charm*). For you—I would do much more . . . Well, that is what I came for. I must go.

Beneatha. Will you call me Monday?

Asagai. Yes . . . We have a great deal to talk about. I mean about identity and time and all that.

Beneatha. Time?

Asagai. Yes. About how much time one needs to know what one feels.

Beneatha. You never understood that there is more than one kind of feeling which can exist between a man and a woman—or, at least, there should be.

Asagai (*shaking his head negatively but gently*). No. Between a man and a woman there need be only one kind of feeling. I have that for you . . . Now even . . . right this moment . . .

Beneatha. I know—and by itself—it won't do. I can find that anywhere.

Asagai. For a woman it should be enough.

Beneatha. I know—because that's what it says in all the novels that men write. But it isn't. Go ahead and laugh—but I'm not interested in being someone's little episode in America or—(*with *feminine vengeance)*—one of them! (Asagai *has burst into laughter again.*) That's funny, huh!

Asagai. It's just that every American girl I have known has said that to me. White—black—in this you are all the same. And the same speech, too!

Beneatha (*angrily*). Yuk, yuk, yuk!

Asagai. It's how you can be sure that the world's most liberated women are not liberated at all. You all talk about it too much!

(Mama *enters and is immediately all social charm because of the presence of a guest.*)

Beneatha. Oh—Mama—this is Mr. Asagai.

Mama. How do you do?

Asagai (*total politeness to an elder*). How do you do, Mrs. Younger. Please forgive me for coming at such an outrageous hour on a Saturday.

Mama. Well, you are quite welcome. I just hope you understand that our house don't always look like this. (*chatterish*) You must come again. I would love to hear all about—(*not sure of the name*)—your country. I think it's so sad the way our American Negroes don't know nothing about Africa 'cept Tarzan and all that. And all that money they pour into these churches when they ought to be helping you people over there drive out them French and Englishmen done taken away your land.

(*The mother flashes a slightly superior look at her daughter upon completion of the recitation.*)

Asagai (*taken aback by this sudden and acutely unrelated expression of sympathy*). Yes . . . yes . . .

Mama (*smiling at him suddenly and relaxing and looking* *him over*). How many miles is it from here to where you come from?

Asagai. Many thousands.

Mama (*looking at him as she would* Walter). I bet you don't half look after yourself, being away from your mama, either. I spec you better come 'round here from time to time and get yourself some decent home-cooked meals . . .

Asagai (*moved*). Thank you. Thank you very much. (*They are all quiet, then—*) Well . . . I must go. I will call you Monday, Alaiyo.

Mama. What's that he call you?

Asagai. Oh—"Alaiyo." I hope you don't mind. It is what you would call a nickname, I think. It is a Yoruba word. I am a Yoruba.

Mama (*looking at* Beneatha). I—I thought he was from—

Asagai (*understanding*). Nigeria is my country. Yoruba is my tribal origin—

Beneatha. You didn't tell us what Alaiyo means . . . for all I know, you might be calling me Little Idiot or something . . .

Asagai. Well . . . let me see . . . I do not know how just to explain it . . . The sense of a thing can be so different when it changes languages.

Beneatha. You're evading.

Asagai. No—really it is difficult . . . (*thinking*) It means . . . it means One for Whom Bread—Food—Is Not Enough. (*He looks at her.*) Is that all right?

Beneatha (*understanding, softly*). Thank you.

Mama (*looking from one to the other and not understanding any of it*). Well . . . that's nice . . . You must come see us again—Mr.—

Asagai. Ah-sah-guy . . .

Mama. Yes . . . Do come again.

Asagai. Goodbye.

(*He exits.*)

Mama (*after him*). Lord, that's a pretty thing just went out here! (*insinuatingly, to her daughter*) Yes, I guess I see why we done commence to get so interested in Africa 'round here. Missionaries my aunt Jenny!

(*She exits.*)

Beneatha. Oh, Mama! . . .

(*She picks up the Nigerian dress and holds it up to her in front of the mirror again. She sets the headdress on haphazardly and then notices her hair again and clutches at it and then replaces the headdress and frowns at herself. Then she starts to wriggle in front of the mirror as she thinks a Nigerian woman might. Travis enters and regards her.*)

Travis. You cracking up?

Beneatha. Shut up.

(*She pulls the headdress off and looks at herself in the mirror and clutches at her hair again and squinches her eyes as if trying to imagine something. Then, suddenly, she gets her raincoat and kerchief and hurriedly prepares for going out.*)

Mama (*coming back into the room*). She's resting now. Travis, baby, run next door and ask Miss Johnson to please let me have a little kitchen cleanser. This here can is empty as Jacob's kettle.

Travis. I just came in.

Mama. Do as you told. (*He exits and she looks at her daughter.*) Where you going?

Beneatha (*halting at the door*). To become a queen of the Nile!

(*She exits in a breathless blaze of glory.* Ruth *appears in the bedroom doorway.*)

Mama. Who told you to get up?

Ruth. Ain't nothing wrong with me to be lying in no bed for. Where did Bennie go?

Mama (*drumming her fingers*). Far as I could make out— to Egypt. (Ruth *just looks at her.*) What time is it getting to?

Ruth. Ten-twenty. And the mailman going to ring that bell this morning just like he done every morning for the last umpteen years.

(Travis *comes in with the cleanser can.*)

Travis. She say to tell you that she don't have much.

Mama (*angrily*). Lord, some people I could name sure is tight-fisted! (*directing her grandson*) Mark two cans of cleanser down on the list there. If she that hard up for kitchen cleanser, I sure don't want to forget to get her none!

Ruth. Lena—maybe the woman is just short on cleanser—

Mama (*not listening*).—Much baking powder as she done borrowed from me all these years, she could of done gone into the baking business!

(*The bell sounds suddenly and sharply, and all three are stunned—serious and silent—midspeech. In spite of all the other conversations and distractions of the morning, this is what they have been waiting for, even* Travis, *who looks helplessly from his mother to his grandmother.* Ruth *is the first to come to life again.*)

Ruth (*to* Travis). *Get down them steps, boy!*

(Travis *snaps to life and flies out to get the mail.*)

Mama (*her eyes wide, her hand to her breast*). You mean it done really come?

Ruth (*excited*). Oh, Miss Lena!

Mama (*collecting herself*). Well . . . I don't know what we all so excited about 'round here for. We known it was coming for months.

Ruth. That's a whole lot different from having it come and being able to hold it in your hands . . . a piece of paper worth ten thousand dollars . . . (Travis *bursts back into the room. He holds the envelope high above his head, like a little dancer, his face is radiant and he is breathless. He moves to his grandmother with sudden slow ceremony and puts the envelope into her hands. She accepts it, and then merely holds it and looks at it.*) Come on! Open it . . . Lord have mercy, I wish Walter Lee was here!

Travis. Open it, Grandmama!

Mama (*staring at it*). Now you all be quiet. It's just a check.

Ruth. Open it . . .

Mama (*still staring at it*). Now don't act silly . . . We ain't never been no people to act silly 'bout no money—

Ruth (*swiftly*). We ain't never had none before—*open it!*

(Mama *finally makes a good strong tear and pulls out the thin blue slice of paper and inspects it closely. The boy and his mother study it raptly over* Mama's *shoulders.*)

Mama. *Travis!* (*She is counting off with doubt.*) Is that the right number of zeros?

Travis. Yes'm . . . ten thousand dollars. Gaalee, Grandmama, you rich.

Mama (*She holds the check away from her, still looking at it. Slowly her face sobers into a mask of unhappiness.*). Ten thousand dollars. (*She hands it to* Ruth.) Put it away somewhere, Ruth. (*She does not look at* Ruth; *her eyes seem to be seeing something somewhere very far off.*) Ten thousand dollars.

Travis (*to his mother, sincerely*). What's the matter with Grandmama—don't she want to be rich?

Ruth (*distractedly*). You go on out and play now, baby. (Travis *exits.* Mama *starts wiping dishes absently, humming intently to herself.* Ruth *turns to her, with kind exasperation.*) You've gone and got yourself upset.

Mama (*not looking at her*). I spec if it wasn't for you all . . . I would just put that money away or give it to the church or something.

Ruth. Now what kind of talk is that. Mr. Younger would just be plain mad if he could hear you talking foolish like that.

Mama (*stopping and staring off*). Yes . . . he sure would. (*sighing*) We got enough to do with that money, all right. (*She halts then, and turns and looks at her daughter-in-law hard;* Ruth *avoids her eyes and* Mama *wipes her hands with finality and starts to speak firmly to* Ruth.) Where did you go today, girl?

Ruth. To the doctor.

Mama (*impatiently*). Now, Ruth . . . you know better than that. Old Doctor Jones is strange enough in his way but there ain't nothing 'bout him make somebody slip and call him "she"—like you done this morning.

Ruth. Well, that's what happened—my tongue slipped.

Mama. You went to see that woman, didn't you?

Ruth (*defensively, giving herself away*). What woman you talking about?

Mama (*angrily*). That woman who—

(Walter *enters in great excitement.*)

Walter. Did it come?

Mama (*quietly*). Can't you give people a Christian greeting before you start asking about money?

Walter (*to Ruth*). Did it come? (Ruth *unfolds the check and lays it quietly before him, watching him intently with thoughts of her own.* Walter *sits down and grasps it close and counts off the zeros.*) Ten thousand dollars—(*He turns suddenly, frantically to his mother and draws some papers out of his breast pocket.*) Mama—look. Old Willy Harris put everything on paper—

Mama. Son—I think you ought to talk to your wife . . . I'll go on out and leave you alone if you want—

Walter. I can talk to her later—Mama, look—

Mama. Son—

Walter. WILL SOMEBODY PLEASE LISTEN TO ME TODAY!

Mama (*quietly*). I don't 'low no yellin' in this house, Walter Lee, and you know it—(Walter *stares at them in frustration and starts to speak several times.*) And there ain't going to be no investing in no liquor stores. I don't aim to have to speak on that again.

(*a long pause*)

Walter. Oh—so you don't aim to have to speak on that again? So *you* have decided . . . (*crumpling his papers*) Well, *you* tell that to my boy tonight when you put him to sleep on the living-room couch . . . (*turning to* Mama *and speaking directly to her*) Yeah— and tell it to my wife, Mama, tomorrow when she has to go out of here to look after somebody else's kids. And tell it to *me*, Mama, every time we need a new pair of curtains, and I have to watch *you* go out and work in somebody's kitchen. Yeah, you tell me then!

(Walter *starts out.*)

Ruth. Where you going?

Walter. I'm going out!

Ruth. Where?

Walter. Just out of this house somewhere—

Ruth (*getting her coat*). I'll come too.

Walter. I don't want you to come!

Ruth. I got something to talk to you about, Walter.

Walter. That's too bad.

Mama (*still quietly*). Walter Lee—(*She waits and he finally turns and looks at her.*) Sit down.

Walter. I'm a grown man, Mama.

Mama. Ain't nobody said you wasn't grown. But you still in my house and my presence. And as long as you are—you'll talk to your wife civil. Now sit down.

Ruth (*suddenly*). Oh, let him go on out and drink himself to death! He makes me sick to my stomach! (*She flings her coat against him.*)

Walter (*violently*). And you turn mine too, baby! (Ruth *goes into their bedroom and slams the door behind her.*) That was my greatest mistake—

Mama (*still quietly*). Walter, what is the matter with you?

Walter. Matter with me? Ain't nothing the matter with *me!*

Mama. Yes there is. Something eating you up like a crazy man. Something more than me not giving you this money. The past few years I been watching it happen to you. You get all nervous acting and kind of wild in the eyes—(Walter *jumps up impatiently at her words.*) I said sit there now, I'm talking to you!

Walter. Mama—I don't need no nagging at me today.

Mama. Seem like you getting to a place where you always tied up in some kind of knot about something. But if anybody ask you 'bout it you just yell at 'em and bust out the house and go out and drink somewheres. Walter Lee, people can't live with that. Ruth's a good, patient girl in her way—but you getting to be too much. Boy, don't make the mistake of driving that girl away from you.

Walter. Why—what she do for me?

Mama. She loves you.

Walter. Mama—I'm going out. I want to go off somewhere and be by myself for a while.

Mama. I'm sorry 'bout your liquor store, son. It just wasn't the thing for us to do. That's what I want to tell you about—

Walter. I got to go out, Mama—

(*He rises.*)

Mama. It's dangerous, son.

Walter. What's dangerous?

Mama. When a man goes outside his home to look for peace.

Walter (*beseechingly*). Then why can't there never be no peace in this house then?

Mama. You done found it in some other house?

Walter. No—there ain't no woman! Why do women always think there's a woman somewhere when a man gets restless. (*coming to her*) Mama—Mama—I want so many things . . .

Mama. Yes, son—

Walter. I want so many things that they are driving me kind of crazy . . . Mama—look at me.

Mama. I'm looking at you. You a good-looking boy. You got a job, a nice wife, a fine boy and—

Walter. A job. (*looks at her*) Mama, a job? I open and close car doors all day long. I drive a man around in his limousine and I say, "Yes, sir; no, sir; very good, sir; shall I take the Drive, sir?" Mama, that ain't no kind of job . . . that ain't nothing at all. (*very quietly*) Mama, I don't know if I can make you understand.

Mama. Understand what, baby?

Walter (*quietly*). Sometimes it's like I can see the future stretched out in front of me—just plain as day. The future, Mama. Hanging over there at the edge of my days. Just waiting for me—a big, looming blank space—full of *nothing*. Just waiting for *me*. (*pause*) Mama—sometimes when I'm downtown and I pass them cool, quiet-looking restaurants where them white boys are sitting back and talking 'bout things . . . sitting there turning deals worth millions of dollars . . . sometimes I see guys don't look much older than me—

Mama. Son—how come you talk so much 'bout money?

Walter (*with immense passion*). Because it is life, Mama!

Mama (*quietly*). Oh—(*very quietly*) So now it's life. Money is life. Once upon a time freedom used to be life—now it's money. I guess the world really do change . . .

Walter. No—it was always money, Mama. We just didn't know about it.

Mama. No . . . something has changed. (*She looks at him.*) You something new, boy. In my time we was worried about not being lynched and getting to the North if we could and how to stay alive and still have a pinch of dignity too . . . Now here come you and Beneatha—talking 'bout things we ain't never even thought about hardly, me and your daddy. You ain't satisfied or proud of nothing we done. I mean that you had a home; that we kept you out of trouble till you was grown; that you don't have to ride to work on the back of nobody's streetcar—You my children—but how different we done become.

Walter. You just don't understand, Mama, you just don't understand.

Mama. Son—do you know your wife is expecting another baby? (*Walter stands, stunned, and absorbs what his mother has said.*) That's what she wanted to talk to you about. (Walter *sinks down into a chair.*) This ain't for me to be telling—but you ought to know. (*She waits.*) I think Ruth is thinking 'bout getting rid of that child.

Walter (*slowly understanding*). No—no—Ruth wouldn't do that.

Mama. When the world gets ugly enough—a woman will do anything for her family. *The part that's already living.*

Walter. You don't know Ruth, Mama, if you think she would do that.

(Ruth *opens the bedroom door and stands there a little limp.*)

Ruth (*beaten*). Yes I would too, Walter. (*pause*) I gave her a five-dollar down payment.

(*There is total silence as the man stares at his wife and the mother stares at her son.*)

Mama (*presently*). Well—(*tightly*) Well—son, I'm waiting to hear you say something . . . I'm waiting to hear how you be your father's son. Be the man he was . . . (*pause*) Your wife say she going to destroy your child. And I'm waiting to hear you talk like him and say we a people who give children life, not who destroys them—(*She rises.*) I'm waiting to see you stand up and look like your daddy and say we done give up one baby to poverty and that we ain't going to give up nary another one . . . I'm waiting.

Walter. Ruth—

Mama. If you a son of mine, tell her! (Walter *turns, looks at her and can say nothing. She continues, bitterly.*) You . . . you are a disgrace to your father's memory. Somebody get me my hat.

Act TWO

Scene 1 *Later the same day*

> Ruth *is ironing again. She has the radio going. Presently* Beneatha's *bedroom door opens and* Ruth's *mouth falls, and she puts down the iron in fascination.*

Ruth. What have we got on tonight!

Beneatha (*emerging grandly from the doorway so that we can see her thoroughly robed in the costume* Asagai *brought*). You are looking at what a well-dressed Nigerian woman wears—(*She parades for* Ruth, *her hair completely hidden by the headdress; she is coquettishly fanning herself with an ornate oriental fan, mistakenly more like Butterfly than any Nigerian that ever was.*) Isn't it beautiful? (*She promenades to the radio and, with an arrogant flourish, turns off the good loud blues that is playing.*) Enough of this assimilationist junk! (Ruth *follows her with her eyes as she goes to the phonograph and puts on a record and turns and waits ceremoniously for the music to come up. Then, with a shout—*) OCOMOGOSIAY!

(Ruth *jumps. The music comes up, a lovely Nigerian melody.* Beneatha *listens, enraptured, her eyes far away—"back to the past." She begins to dance.* Ruth *is dumbfounded.*)

Ruth. What kind of dance is that?

Beneatha. A folk dance.

Ruth (*Pearl Bailey*). What kind of folks do that, honey?

Beneatha. It's from Nigeria. It's a dance of welcome.

Ruth. Who you welcoming?

Beneatha. The men back to the village.

Ruth. Where they been?

Beneatha. How should I know—out hunting or something. Anyway, they are coming back now . . .

Ruth. Well, that's good.

Beneatha (*with the record*).
Alundi, alundi
Alundi alunya
Jop pu a jeepua
Ang gu soooooooooo
Ai yai yae . . .
Ayehaye—alundi . . .

(*Walter comes in during this performance; he has obviously been drinking. He leans against the door heavily and watches his sister, at first with distaste. Then his eyes look off—"back to the past"—as he lifts both his fists to the roof, screaming.*)

Walter. YEAH . . . AND ETHIOPIA STRETCH FORTH HER HANDS AGAIN!

Ruth (*drily, looking at him*). Yes—and Africa sure is claiming her own tonight. (*She gives them both up and starts ironing again.*)

Walter (*all in a dramatic shout*). Shut up! . . . I'm digging them drums . . . them drums move me! . . . (*He makes his way to his wife's face and leans in close to her.*) In my *heart of hearts*—(*He thumps his chest.*)—I am much warrior!

Ruth (*without even looking up*). In your heart of hearts you are much drunkard.

Walter (*coming away from her and starting to wander around* *the room, shouting*). Me and Jomo . . . (*Intently, in his sister's face. She has stopped dancing to watch him in this unknown mood.*) That's my man, Kenyatta. (*shouting and thumping his chest*) FLAMING SPEAR! (*He is suddenly in possession of an imaginary spear and actively spearing enemies all over the room.*) OCOMOGOSIAY . . . THE LION IS WAKING . . . OWIMOWEH! (*He pulls his shirt open and leaps up on a table and gestures with his spear. The bell rings.* Ruth *goes to answer.*)

Beneatha (*to encourage* Walter, *thoroughly caught up with this side of him*). OCOMOGOSIAY, FLAMING SPEAR!

Walter (*On the table, very far gone, his eyes pure glass sheets. He sees what we cannot, that he is a leader of his people, a great chief, a descendant of Chaka, and that the hour to march has come*). Listen, my black brothers—

Beneatha. OCOMOGOSIAY!

Walter. —Do you hear the waters rushing against the shores of the coastlands—

Beneatha. OCOMOGOSIAY!

Walter. —Do you hear the screeching of the cocks in yonder hills beyond where the chiefs meet in council for the coming of the mighty war—

Beneatha. OCOMOGOSIAY!

Walter. —Do you hear the beating of the wings of the birds flying low over the mountains and the low places of our land—

(Ruth *opens the door.* George Murchison *enters.*)

Beneatha. OCOMOGOSIAY!

Walter. —Do you hear the singing of the women, singing the war songs of our fathers to the babies in the great houses . . . singing the sweet war songs? OH, DO YOU HEAR, MY BLACK BROTHERS!

Beneatha (*completely gone*). We hear you, Flaming Spear—

Walter. Telling us to prepare for the greatness of the time— (*to George*) Black Brother!

(*He extends his hand for the fraternal clasp.*)

George. Black Brother, hell!

Ruth (*having had enough, and embarrassed for the family*). Beneatha, you got company—what's the matter with you? Walter Lee Younger, get down off that table and stop acting like a fool . . .

(*Walter comes down off the table suddenly and makes a quick exit to the bathroom.*)

Ruth. He's had a little to drink . . . I don't know what her excuse is.

George (*to Beneatha*). Look honey, we're going *to* the theatre—we're not going to be *in* it . . . so go change, huh?

Ruth. You expect this boy to go out with you looking like that?

Beneatha (*looking at George*). That's up to George. If he's ashamed of his heritage—

George. Oh, don't be so proud of yourself, Bennie—just because you look eccentric.

Beneatha. How can something that's natural be eccentric?

George. That's what being eccentric means—being natural. Get dressed.

Beneatha. I don't like that, George.

Ruth. Why must you and your brother make an argument out of everything people say?

Beneatha. Because I hate assimilationist Negroes!

Ruth. Will somebody please tell me what assimila-whoever means!

George. Oh, it's just a college girl's way of calling people Uncle Toms—but that isn't what it means at all.

Ruth. Well, what does it mean?

Beneatha (*cutting* George *off and staring at him as she replies to* Ruth). It means someone who is willing to give up his own culture and submerge himself completely in the dominant, and in this case, *oppressive* culture!

George. Oh, dear, dear, dear! Here we go! A lecture on the African past! On our Great West African Heritage! In one second we will hear all about the great Ashanti empires; the great Songhay civilizations; and the great sculpture of Bénin—and then some poetry in the Bantu—and the whole monologue will end with the word *heritage!* (*nastily*) Let's face it, baby, your heritage is nothing but a bunch of raggedy spirituals and some grass huts!

Beneatha. *Grass huts!* (Ruth *crosses to her and forcibly pushes her toward the bedroom.*) See there . . . you are standing there in your splendid ignorance talking about people who were the first to smelt iron on the face of the earth! (Ruth *is pushing her through the door.*) The Ashanti were performing surgical operations when the English—(Ruth *pulls the door to, with* Beneatha *on the other side, and smiles graciously at* George. Beneatha *opens the door and shouts the end of the sentence defiantly at* George.)—were still tattooing themselves with blue dragons . . . (*She goes back inside.*)

Ruth. Have a seat, George. (*They both sit. Ruth folds her hands rather primly on her lap, determined to demonstrate the civilization of the family.*) Warm, ain't it? I mean for September. (*pause*) Just like they always say about Chicago weather: If it's too hot or cold for you, just wait a minute and it'll change. (*She smiles happily at this cliché of clichés.*) Everybody say it's got to do with them bombs and things they keep setting off. (*pause*) Would you like a nice cold beer?

George. No, thank you. I don't care for beer. (*He looks at his watch.*) I hope she hurries up.

Ruth. What time is the show?

George. It's an eight-thirty curtain. That's just Chicago, though. In New York standard curtain time is eight-forty.

(*He is rather proud of this knowledge.*)

Ruth (*properly appreciating it*). You get to New York a lot?

George (*offhand*). Few times a year.

Ruth. Oh—that's nice. I've never been to New York.

(*Walter enters. We feel he has relieved himself, but the edge of unreality is still with him.*)

Walter. New York ain't got nothing Chicago ain't. Just a bunch of hustling people all squeezed up together—being "Eastern."

(*He twists his face in displeasure.*)

George. Oh—you've been?

Walter. *Plenty* of times.

Ruth (*shocked at the lie*). Walter Lee Younger!

Walter (*staring her down*). Plenty! (*pause*) What we got to drink in this house? Why don't you offer this man some refreshment. (*to* George) They don't know how to entertain people in this house, man.

George. Thank you—I don't really care for anything.

Walter (*feeling his head; sobriety coming*). Where's Mama?

Ruth. She ain't come back yet.

Walter (*looking* Murchison *over from head to toe, scrutinizing his carefully casual tweed sports jacket over cashmere V-neck sweater over soft eyelet shirt and tie, and soft slacks, finished off with white buckskin shoes*). Why all you college boys wear them fairyish-looking white shoes?

Ruth. Walter Lee!

(George Murchison *ignores the remark.*)

Walter (*to* Ruth). Well, they look crazy as hell—white shoes, cold as it is.

Ruth (*crushed*). You have to excuse him—

Walter. No he don't! Excuse me for what? What you always excusing me for! I'll excuse myself when I needs to be excused! (*a pause*) They look as funny as them black knee socks Beneatha wears out of here all the time.

Ruth. It's the college *style,* Walter.

Walter. Style, hell! She looks like she got burnt legs or something!

Ruth. Oh, Walter—

Walter (*an irritable mimic*). Oh, Walter! Oh, Walter! (*to*

Murchison) How's your old man making out? I understand you all going to buy that big hotel on the Drive? (*He finds a beer in the refrigerator, wanders over to* Murchison, *sipping and wiping his lips with the back of his hand, and straddling a chair backwards to talk to the other man.*) Shrewd move. Your old man is all right, man. (*tapping his head and half winking for emphasis*) I mean he knows how to operate. I mean he thinks *big*, you know what I mean, I mean for a *home*, you know? But I think he's kind of running out of ideas now. I'd like to talk to him. Listen, man, I got some plans that could turn this city upside down. I mean I think like he does. *Big.* Invest big, gamble big, hell, lose *big* if you have to, you know what I mean. It's hard to find a man on this whole South Side who understands my kind of thinking—you dig? (*He scrutinizes* Murchison *again, drinks his beer, squints his eyes and leans in close, confidential, man to man.*) Me and you ought to sit down and talk sometimes, man. Man, I got me some ideas . . .

Murchison (*with boredom*). Yeah—sometimes we'll have to do that, Walter.

Walter (*understanding the indifference, and offended*). Yeah—well, when you get the time, man. I know you a busy little boy.

Ruth. Walter, please—

Walter (*bitterly, hurt*). I know ain't nothing in this world as busy as you black college boys with your fraternity pins and white shoes . . .

Ruth (*covering her face with humiliation*). Oh, Walter Lee—

Walter. I see you all all the time—with the books tucked under your arms—going to your (*British A—*

a mimic) "clahsses." And for what! What the hell you learning over there? Filling up your heads— (*counting off on his fingers*)—with the sociology and the psychology—but they teaching you how to be a man? How to take over and run the world? They teaching you how to run a rubber plantation or a steel mill? Naw—just to talk proper and read books and wear white shoes . . .

George (*looking at him with distaste, a little above it all*). You're all wacked up with bitterness, man.

Walter (*intently, almost quietly, between the teeth, glaring at the boy*). And you—ain't you bitter, man? Ain't you just about had it yet? Don't you see no stars gleaming that you can't reach out and grab? You happy? You got it made? Bitter? Man, I'm a volcano. Bitter? Here I am a giant—surrounded by ants! Ants who can't even understand what it is the giant is talking about.

Ruth (*passionately and suddenly*). Oh, Walter—ain't you with nobody!

Walter (*violently*). No! 'Cause ain't nobody with me! Not even my own mother!

Ruth. Walter, that's a terrible thing to say!

(Beneatha *enters, dressed for the evening in a cocktail dress and earrings.*)

George. Well—hey, you look great.

Beneatha. Let's go, George. See you all later.

Ruth. Have a nice time.

George. Thanks. Good night. (*to* Walter, *sarcastically*) Good night, *Prometheus.*

(Beneatha *and* George *exit.*)

Walter (*to* Ruth). Who is Prometheus?

Ruth. I don't know. Don't worry about it.

Walter (*in fury, pointing after* George). See there—they get to a point where they can't insult you man to man—they got to go talk about something ain't nobody never heard of!

Ruth. How do you know it was an insult? (*to humor him*) Maybe Prometheus is a nice fellow.

Walter. Prometheus! I bet there ain't even no such thing! I bet that simple-minded clown—

Ruth. Walter—

(*She stops what she is doing and looks at him.*)

Walter (*yelling*). Don't start!

Ruth. Start what?

Walter. Your nagging! Where was I? Who was I with? How much money did I spend?

Ruth (*plaintively*). Walter Lee—why don't we just try to talk about it . . .

Walter (*not listening*). I been out talking with people who understand me. People who care about the things I got on my mind.

Ruth (*wearily*). I guess that means people like Willy Harris.

Walter. Yes, people like Willy Harris.

Ruth (*with a sudden flash of impatience*). Why don't you all just hurry up and go into the banking business and stop talking about it!

Walter. Why? You want to know why? 'Cause we all tied up in a race of people that don't know how to do nothing but moan, pray, and have babies!

(*The line is too bitter even for him, and he looks at her and sits down.*)

Ruth. Oh, Walter . . . (*softly*) Honey, why can't you stop fighting me?

Walter (*without thinking*). Who's fighting you? Who even cares about you?

(*This line begins the retardation of his mood.*)

Ruth. Well—(*She waits a long time, and then with resignation starts to put away her things.*) I guess I might as well go on to bed . . . (*more or less to herself*) I don't know where we lost it . . . but we have . . . (*then, to him*) I— I'm sorry about this new baby, Walter. I guess maybe I better go on and do what I started . . . I guess I just didn't realize how bad things was with us . . . I guess I just didn't really realize—(*She starts out to the bedroom and stops.*) You want some hot milk?

Walter. Hot milk?

Ruth. Yes—hot milk.

Walter. Why hot milk?

Ruth. 'Cause after all that liquor you come home with, you ought to have something hot in your stomach.

Walter. I don't want no milk.

Ruth. You want some coffee then?

Walter. No, I don't want no coffee. I don't want nothing hot to drink. (*almost plaintively*) Why you always trying to give me something to eat?

Ruth (*standing and looking at him helplessly*). What else can I give you, Walter Lee Younger?

(*She stands and looks at him and presently turns to go out again. He lifts his head and watches her going away from him in a new mood that began to emerge when he asked her "Who cares about you?"*)

Walter. It's been rough, ain't it, baby? (*She hears and stops but does not turn around, and he continues to her back.*) I guess between two people there ain't never as much understood as folks generally thinks there is. I mean like between me and you—(*She turns to face him.*) How we gets to the place where we scared to talk softness to each other. (*He waits, thinking hard himself.*) Why you think it got to be like that? (*He is thoughtful, almost as a child would be.*) Ruth, what is it gets into people ought to be close?

Ruth. I don't know, honey. I think about it a lot.

Walter. On account of you and me, you mean? The way things are with us. The way something done come down between us.

Ruth. There ain't so much between us, Walter . . . Not when you come to me and try to talk to me. Try to be with me . . . a little even.

Walter (*total honesty*). Sometimes . . . sometimes . . . I don't even know how to try.

Ruth. Walter—

Walter. Yes?

Ruth (*coming to him, gently and with misgiving, but coming to him*). Honey . . . life don't have to be like this. I mean sometimes people can do things so that things are better . . . You remember how we used to talk when Travis was born . . . about the way we were going to live . . . the kind of house . . . (*She is stroking his head.*) Well, it's all starting to slip away from us . . .

(Mama *enters, and* Walter *jumps up and shouts at her.*)

Walter. Mama, where have you been?

Mama. My—them steps is longer than they used to be. Whew! (*She sits down and ignores him.*) How you feeling this evening, Ruth?

(Ruth *shrugs, disturbed some at having been prematurely interrupted and watching her husband knowingly.*)

Walter. Mama, where have you been all day?

Mama (*still ignoring him and leaning on the table and changing to more comfortable shoes*). Where's Travis?

Ruth. I let him go out earlier and he ain't come back yet. Boy, is he going to get it!

Walter. Mama!

Mama (*as if she has heard him for the first time*). Yes, son?

Walter. Where did you go this afternoon?

Mama. I went downtown to tend to some business that I had to tend to.

Walter. What kind of business?

Mama. You know better than to question me like a child, Brother.

Walter (*rising and bending over the table*). Where were you, Mama? (*bringing his fists down and shouting*) Mama, you didn't go do something with that insurance money, something crazy?

(*The front door opens slowly, interrupting him, and* Travis *peeks his head in, less than hopefully.*)

Travis (*to his mother*). Mama, I—

Ruth. "Mama I" nothing! You're going to get it, boy! Get on in that bedroom and get yourself ready!

Travis. But I—

Mama. Why don't you all never let the child explain hisself.

Ruth. Keep out of it now, Lena.

(Mama *clamps her lips together, and* Ruth *advances toward her son menacingly.*)

Ruth. A thousand times I have told you not to go off like that—

Mama (*holding out her arms to her grandson*). Well—at least let me tell him something. I want him to be the first one to hear . . . Come here, Travis. (*The boy obeys, gladly.*) Travis—(*She takes him by the shoulder and looks into his face.*)—you know that money we got in the mail this morning?

Travis. Yes'm—

Mama. Well—what you think your grandmama gone and done with that money?

Travis. I don't know, Grandmama.

Mama (*putting her finger on his nose for emphasis*). She went out and she bought you a house! (*The explosion comes from* Walter *at the end of the revelation, and he jumps up and turns away from all of them in a fury.* Mama *continues, to* Travis.) You glad about the house? It's going to be yours when you get to be a man.

Travis. Yeah—I always wanted to live in a house.

Mama. All right, gimme some sugar then—(Travis *puts his arms around her neck as she watches her son over the boy's shoulder. Then, to* Travis, *after the embrace.*) Now when you say your prayers tonight, you thank God and your grandfather—'cause it was him who give you the house—in his way.

Ruth (*taking the boy from* Mama *and pushing him toward the bedroom*). Now you get out of here and get ready for your beating.

Travis. Aw, Mama—

Ruth. Get on in there—(*closing the door behind him and turning radiantly to her mother-in-law*) So you went and did it!

Mama (*quietly, looking at her son with pain*). Yes, I did.

Ruth (*raising both arms classically*). *Praise God!* (*Looks at* Walter *a moment, who says nothing. She crosses rapidly to her husband.*) Please, honey—let me be glad . . . you be glad too. (*She has laid her hands on his shoulders, but he shakes himself free of her roughly, without turning to face her.*) Oh, Walter . . . a home . . . *a home.* (*She comes back to* Mama.) Well—where is it? How big is it? How much it going to cost?

Mama. Well—

Ruth. When we moving?

Mama (*smiling at her*). First of the month.

Ruth (*throwing back her head with jubilance*). *Praise God!*

Mama (*tentatively, still looking at her son's back turned against her and* Ruth). It's—it's a nice house too . . . (*She cannot help speaking directly to him. An imploring quality in her voice, her manner, makes her almost like a girl now.*) Three bedrooms—nice big one for you and Ruth . . . Me and Beneatha still have to share our room, but Travis have one of his own—and (*with difficulty*) I figure if the—new baby—is a boy, we could get one of them double-decker outfits . . . And there's a yard with a little patch of dirt where I could maybe get to grow me a few flowers . . . And a nice big basement . . .

Ruth. Walter honey, be glad—

Mama (*still to his back, fingering things on the table*). 'Course I don't want to make it sound fancier than it is . . . It's just a plain little old house—but it's made good and solid—and it will be *ours*. Walter Lee—it makes a difference in a man when he can walk on floors that belong to *him* . . .

Ruth. Where is it?

Mama (*frightened at this telling*). Well—well—it's out there in Clybourne Park—

(Ruth's *radiance fades abruptly, and* Walter *finally turns slowly to face his mother with incredulity and hostility.*)

Ruth. Where?

Mama (*matter-of-factly*). Four o six Clybourne Street, Clybourne Park.

Ruth. Clybourne Park? Mama, there ain't no black people living in Clybourne Park.

Mama (*almost idiotically*). Well, I guess there's going to be some now.

Walter (*bitterly*). So that's the peace and comfort you went out and bought for us today!

Mama (*raising her eyes to meet his finally*). Son—I just tried to find the nicest place for the least amount of money for my family.

Ruth (*trying to recover from the shock*). Well—well—'course I ain't one never been 'fraid of no crackers, mind you—but—well, wasn't there no other houses nowhere?

Mama. Them houses they put up for blacks in them areas way out all seem to cost twice as much as other houses. I did the best I could.

Ruth (*Struck senseless with the news, in its various degrees of goodness and trouble, she sits a moment, her fists propping her chin in thought, and then she starts to rise, bringing her fists down with vigor, the radiance spreading from cheek to cheek again.*). Well—well!—All I can say is—if this is my time in life—*my time*—to say goodbye—(*And she builds with momentum as she starts to circle the room with an exuberant, almost tearfully happy release.*)—to these cracking walls!—(*She pounds the walls.*)—and these marching roaches!— (*She wipes at an imaginary army of marching roaches.*)—and this cramped little closet which ain't now or never was no kitchen! . . . then I say it loud and good, *Hallelujah! and goodbye misery . . . I don't never want to see your ugly face again!* (*She laughs joyously, having practically destroyed the apartment, and flings her arms up and lets them come down happily, slowly, reflectively, over her abdomen, aware for the first time perhaps that the life therein pulses with happiness and not despair.*) Lena?

Mama (*moved, watching her happiness*). Yes, honey?

Ruth (*looking off*). Is there—is there a whole lot of sunlight?

Mama (*understanding*). Yes, child, there's a whole lot of sunlight.

(*long pause*)

Ruth (*collecting herself and going to the door of the room Travis is in*). Well—I guess I better see 'bout Travis. (*to* Mama) Lord, I sure don't feel like whipping nobody today!

(*She exits.*)

Mama (*The mother and son are left alone now and the mother waits a long time, considering deeply, before she* *speaks.*). Son—you—you understand what I done, don't you? (Walter *is silent and sullen.*) I—I just seen my family falling apart today . . . just falling to pieces in front of my eyes . . . We couldn't of gone on like we was today. We was going backwards 'stead of forwards—talking 'bout killing babies and wishing each other was dead . . . When it gets like that in life—you just got to do something different, push on out and do something bigger . . . (*She waits.*) I wish you say something, son . . . I wish you'd say how deep inside you you think I done the right thing—

Walter (*crossing slowly to his bedroom door and finally turning there and speaking measuredly*). What you need me to say you done right for? *You* the head of this family. You run our lives like you want to. It was your money and you did what you wanted with it. So what you need for me to say it was all right for? (*bitterly, to hurt her as deeply as he knows is possible*) So you butchered up a dream of mine—you—who always talking 'bout your children's dreams . . .

Mama. Walter Lee—

(*He just closes the door behind him. Mama sits alone, thinking heavily.*)

Scene 2 *Friday night. A few weeks later*

> Packing crates mark the intention of the family to move. Beneatha and George come in, presumably from an evening out again.

George. OK . . . OK, whatever you say . . . (*They both sit on the couch. He tries to kiss her. She moves away.*) Look, we've had a nice evening; let's not spoil it, huh? . . .

(*He again turns her head and tries to nuzzle in and she turns away from him, not with distaste but with momentary lack of interest, in a mood to pursue what they were talking about.*)

Beneatha. I'm *trying* to talk to you.

George. We always talk.

Beneatha. Yes—and I love to talk.

George (*exasperated, rising*). I know it and I don't mind it sometimes . . . I want you to cut it out, see—The moody stuff, I mean. I don't like it. You're a nice-looking girl . . . all over. That's all you need, honey, forget the atmosphere. Guys aren't going to go for the atmosphere—they're going to go for what they see. Be glad for that. Drop the Garbo routine. It doesn't go with you. As for myself, I want a nice—(*groping*)—simple (*thoughtfully*)—sophisticated girl . . . not a poet—OK?

(*She rebuffs him again and he starts to leave.*)

Beneatha. Why are you angry?

George. Because this is stupid! I don't go out with you to discuss the nature of "quiet desperation" or to hear all about your thoughts—because the world will go on thinking what it thinks regardless—

Beneatha. Then why read books? Why go to school?

George (*with artificial patience, counting on his fingers*). It's simple. You read books—to learn facts—to get grades—to pass the course—to get a degree. That's all—it has nothing to do with thoughts.

(*a long pause*)

Beneatha. I see. (*a longer pause as she looks at him*) Good night, George.

(George *looks at her a little oddly and starts to exit. He meets* Mama *coming in.*)

George. Oh—hello, Mrs. Younger.

Mama. Hello, George, how you feeling?

George. Fine—fine, how are you?

Mama. Oh, a little tired. You know them steps can get you after a day's work. You all have a nice time tonight?

George. Yes—a fine time. Well, good night.

Mama. Good night. (*He exits.* Mama *closes the door behind her.*) Hello, honey. What you sitting like that for?

Beneatha. I'm just sitting.

Mama. Didn't you have a nice time?

Beneatha. No.

Mama. No? What's the matter?

Beneatha. Mama, George is a fool—honest.

(*She rises.*)

Mama (*Hustling around unloading the packages she has entered with. She stops.*). Is he, baby?

Beneatha. Yes.

(Beneatha *makes up* Travis's *bed as she talks.*)

Mama. You sure?

Beneatha. Yes.

Mama. Well—I guess you better not waste your time with no fools.

(Beneatha *looks up at her mother, watching her put groceries in the refrigerator. Finally she gathers up her things and starts into the bedroom. At the door she stops and looks back at her mother.)*

Beneatha. Mama—

Mama. Yes, baby—

Beneatha. Thank you.

Mama. For what?

Beneatha. For understanding me this time.

(She exits quickly and the mother stands, smiling a little, looking at the place where Beneatha *just stood.* Ruth *enters.)*

Ruth. Now don't you fool with any of this stuff, Lena—

Mama. Oh, I just thought I'd sort a few things out.

(The phone rings. Ruth *answers.)*

Ruth *(at the phone).* Hello—Just a minute. *(goes to door)* Walter, it's Mrs. Arnold. *(Waits. Goes back to the phone. Tense.)* Hello. Yes, this is his wife speaking . . . He's lying down now. Yes . . . well, he'll be in tomorrow. He's been very sick. Yes—I know we should have called, but we were so sure he'd be able to come in today. Yes—yes, I'm very sorry. Yes . . . Thank you very much. *(She hangs up.* Walter *is standing in the doorway of the bedroom behind her.)* That was Mrs. Arnold.

Walter *(indifferently).* Was it?

Ruth. She said if you don't come in tomorrow that they are getting a new man . . .

Walter. Ain't that sad—ain't that crying sad.

Ruth. She said Mr. Arnold has had to take a cab for three days . . . Walter, you ain't been to work for three days! *(This is a revelation to her.)* Where you been, Walter Lee Younger? (Walter *looks at her and starts to laugh.*) You're going to lose your job.

Walter. That's right . . .

Ruth. Oh, Walter, and with your mother working like a dog every day—

Walter. That's sad too—Everything is sad.

Mama. What you been doing for these three days, son?

Walter. Mama—you don't know all the things a man what got leisure can find to do in this city . . . What's this—Friday night? Well—Wednesday I borrowed Willy Harris's car and I went for a drive . . . just me and myself and I drove and drove . . . Way out . . . way past South Chicago, and I parked the car and I sat and looked at the steel mills all day long. I just sat in the car and looked at them big black chimneys for hours. Then I drove back and I went to the Green Hat. (*pause*) And Thursday—Thursday I borrowed the car again and I got in it and I pointed it the other way and I drove the other way—for hours—way, way up to Wisconsin, and I looked at the farms. I just drove and looked at the farms. Then I drove back and I went to the Green Hat. (*pause*) And today—today I didn't get the car. Today I just walked. All over the South Side. And I looked at the Negroes and they looked at me, and finally I just sat down on the curb at Thirty-ninth and South Parkway and I just sat there and watched the Negroes go by. And then I went to the Green Hat. You all sad? You all depressed? And you know where I am going right now—

(Ruth *goes out quietly.*)

Mama. Oh, Big Walter, is this the harvest of our days?

Walter. You know what I like about the Green Hat? (*He turns the radio on and a steamy, deep blues pours into the room.*) I like this little cat they got there who blows a sax . . . He blows. He talks to me. He ain't but 'bout five feet tall and he's got a conked head and his eyes is always closed and he's all music—

Mama (*rising and getting some papers out of her handbag*). Walter—

Walter. And there's this other guy who plays the piano . . . and they got a sound. I mean they can work on some music . . . They got the best little combo in the world in the Green Hat . . . You can just sit there and drink and listen to them three men play, and you realize that don't nothing matter worth a damn, but just being there—

Mama. I've helped do it to you, haven't I, son? Walter, I been wrong.

Walter. Naw—you ain't never been wrong about nothing, Mama.

Mama. Listen to me, now. I say I been wrong, son. That I been doing to you what the rest of the world been doing to you. (*She stops, and he looks up slowly at her, and she meets his eyes pleadingly.*) Walter—what you ain't never understood is that I ain't got nothing, don't own nothing, ain't never really wanted nothing that wasn't for you. There ain't nothing as precious to me . . . There ain't nothing worth holding on to, money, dreams, nothing else—if it means—if it means it's going to destroy my boy. (*She puts her papers in front of him, and he watches her without speaking or moving.*) I paid the man thirty-five hundred dollars down on the house. That leaves sixty-five hundred dollars. Monday morning I want you to take this money and take three thousand dollars and put it in a savings account for Beneatha's medical schooling. The rest you put in a checking account—with your name on it. And from now on any penny that come out of it or that go in it is for you to look after. For you to decide. (*She drops her hands a little helplessly.*) It ain't much, but it's all I got in the world, and I'm putting it in your hands. I'm telling you to be the head of this family from now on like you supposed to be.

Walter (*staring at the money*). You trust me like that, Mama?

Mama. I ain't never stop trusting you. Like I ain't never stop loving you.

(*She goes out, and* Walter *sits looking at the money on the table as the music continues in its idiom, pulsing in the room. Finally, in a decisive gesture, he gets up and, in mingled joy and desperation, picks up the money. At the same moment,* Travis *enters for bed.*)

Travis. What's the matter, Daddy? You drunk?

Walter (*sweetly, more sweetly than we have ever known him*). No, Daddy ain't drunk. Daddy ain't going to never be drunk again . . .

Travis. Well, good night, Daddy.

(*The father has come from behind the couch and leans over, embracing his son.*)

Walter. Son, I feel like talking to you tonight.

Travis. About what?

Walter. Oh, about a lot of things. About you and what kind of man you going to be when you grow up . . . Son—son, what do you want to be when you grow up?

Travis. A bus driver.

Walter (*laughing a little*). A what? Man, that ain't nothing to want to be!

Travis. Why not?

Walter. 'Cause, man—it ain't big enough—you know what I mean.

Travis. I don't know then. I can't make up my mind. Sometimes Mama asks me that too. And sometimes when I tell her I just want to be like you—she says she don't want me to be like that and sometimes she says she does . . .

Walter (*gathering him up in his arms*). You know what, Travis? In seven years you going to be seventeen years old. And things is going to be very different with us in seven years, Travis . . . One day when you are seventeen I'll come home—home from my office downtown somewhere—

Travis. You don't work in no office, Daddy.

Walter. No—but after tonight. After what your daddy gonna do tonight, there's going to be offices—a whole lot of offices . . .

Travis. What you gonna do tonight, Daddy?

Walter. You wouldn't understand yet, son, but your daddy's gonna make a transaction . . . a business transaction that's going to change our lives . . . That's how come one day when you 'bout seventeen years old I'll come home and I'll be pretty tired, you know what I mean, after a day of conferences and secretaries getting things wrong the way they do . . . 'cause an executive's life is hell, man—(*The more he talks the farther away he gets.*) And I'll pull the car up on the driveway . . .

just a plain, black Chrysler I think, with whitewalls—no—black tires. More elegant. Rich people don't have to be flashy . . . though I'll have to get something a little sportier for Ruth—maybe a Cadillac convertible to do her shopping in . . . And I'll come up the steps to the house and the gardener will be clipping away at the hedges and he'll say, "Good evening, Mr. Younger." And I'll say, "Hello, Jefferson, how are you this evening?" And I'll go inside and Ruth will come downstairs and meet me at the door and we'll kiss each other and she'll take my arm and we'll go up to your room to see you sitting on the floor with the catalogues of all the great schools in America around you . . . All the great schools in the world! And—and I'll say, all right, son—it's your seventeenth birthday; what is it you've decided? . . . Just tell me where you want to go to school and you'll *go*. Just tell me, what it is you want to be— and you'll *be* it . . . Whatever you want to be—Yessir! (*He holds his arms open for* Travis.) You just name it, son . . . (Travis *leaps into them.*) and I hand you the world!

(Walter's *voice has risen in pitch and hysterical promise, and on the last line he lifts* Travis *high.*)

(*Blackout.*)

Scene 3

Saturday, moving day, one week later.
Before the curtain rises, Ruth's *voice, a*
strident, dramatic church alto, cuts
through the silence.

It is, in the darkness, a triumphant surge, a
penetrating statement of expectation:
"Oh, Lord, I don't feel no ways tired!
Children, oh, glory hallelujah!"

As the curtain rises we see that Ruth *is*
alone in the living room, finishing up the
family's packing. It is moving day. She is
nailing crates and tying cartons. Beneatha
enters, carrying a guitar case, and watches
her exuberant sister-in-law.

Ruth. Hey!

Beneatha (*putting away the case*). Hi.

Ruth (*pointing at a package*). Honey—look in that package there and see what I found on sale this morning at the South Center. (Ruth *gets up and moves to the package and draws out some curtains.*) Lookahere—hand-turned hems!

Beneatha. How do you know the window size out there?

Ruth (*who hadn't thought of that*). Oh—Well, they bound to fit something in the whole house. Anyhow, they was too good a bargain to pass up. (Ruth *slaps her head, suddenly remembering something.*) Oh, Bennie—I meant to put a special note on that carton over there. That's your mama's good china, and she wants 'em to be very careful with it.

Beneatha. I'll do it.

(Beneatha *finds a piece of paper and starts to draw large letters on it.*)

Ruth. You know what I'm going to do soon as I get in that new house?

Beneatha. What?

Ruth. Honey—I'm going to run me a tub of water up to here . . . (*with her fingers practically up to her nostrils*) And I'm going to get in it—and I am going to sit . . . and sit . . . and sit in that hot water and the first person who knocks to tell *me* to hurry up and come out—

Beneatha. Gets shot at sunrise.

Ruth (*laughing happily*). You said it, sister! (*noticing how large* Beneatha *is absent-mindedly making the note*) Honey, they ain't going to read that from no airplane.

Beneatha (*laughing herself*). I guess I always think things have more emphasis if they are big, somehow.

Ruth (*looking up at her and smiling*). You and your brother seem to have that as a philosophy of life. Lord, that man—done changed so 'round here. You know—you know what we did last night? Me and Walter Lee?

Beneatha. What?

Ruth (*smiling to herself*). We went to the movies. (*looking at* Beneatha *to see if she understands*) We went to the movies. You know the last time me and Walter went to the movies together?

Beneatha. No.

Ruth. Me neither. That's how long it been. (*smiling again*) But we went last night. The picture wasn't much good, but that didn't seem to matter. We went—and we held hands.

Beneatha. Oh, Lord!

Ruth. We held hands—and you know what?

Beneatha. What?

Ruth. When we come out of the show it was late and dark and all the stores and things was closed up . . . and it was kind of chilly and there wasn't many people on the streets . . . and we was still holding hands, me and Walter.

Beneatha. You're killing me.

(Walter *enters with a large package. His happiness is deep in him; he cannot keep still with his new-found exuberance. He is singing and wiggling and snapping his fingers. He puts his package in a corner and puts a phonograph record, which he has brought in with him, on the record player. As the music comes up, he dances over to* Ruth *and tries to get her to dance with him. She gives in at last to his raunchiness and in a fit of giggling allows herself to be drawn into his mood and together they deliberately burlesque an old social dance of their youth.*)

Beneatha (*regarding them a long time as they dance, then drawing in her breath for a deeply exaggerated comment which she does not particularly mean*). Talk about—oldddddddddd-fashioneddddddd—Negroes!

Walter (*stopping momentarily*). What kind of Negroes?

(*He says this in fun. He is not angry with her today, nor with anyone. He starts to dance with his wife again.*)

Beneatha. Old-fashioned.

Walter (*as he dances with* Ruth). You know, when these *New Negroes* have their convention—(*pointing at his sister*)—that is going to be the chairman of the Committee on Unending Agitation. (*He goes on dancing, then stops.*) Race, race, race! . . . Girl, I do believe you are the first person in the history of the entire human race to successfully brainwash yourself. (Beneatha *breaks up and he goes on dancing. He stops again, enjoying his tease.*) Damn, even the N double A C P takes a holiday sometimes! (Beneatha *and* Ruth *laugh. He dances with* Ruth *some more and starts to laugh and stops and pantomimes someone over an operating table.*) I can just see that chick someday looking down at some poor cat on an operating table before she starts to slice him, saying . . . (*pulling his sleeves back maliciously*) "By the way, what are your views on civil rights down there? . . ."

(*He laughs at her again and starts to dance happily. The bell sounds.*)

Beneatha. Sticks and stones may break my bones but . . . words will never hurt me!

(Beneatha *goes to the door and opens it as* Walter *and* Ruth *go on with the clowning.* Beneatha *is somewhat surprised to see a quiet-looking middle-aged white man in a business suit holding his hat and a briefcase in his hand and consulting a small piece of paper.*)

Man. Uh—how do you do, miss. I am looking for a Mrs.—(*He looks at the slip of paper.*) Mrs. Lena Younger?

Beneatha (*smoothing her hair with slight embarrassment*). Oh—yes, that's my mother. Excuse me. (*She closes the door and turns to quiet the other two.*) Ruth! Brother! Somebody's here. (*Then she opens the door. The man casts a curious quick glance at all of them.*) Uh—come in please.

Man (*coming in*). Thank you.

Beneatha. My mother isn't here just now. Is it business?

Man. Yes . . . well, of a sort.

Walter (*freely, the Man of the House*). Have a seat. I'm Mrs. Younger's son. I look after most of her business matters.

(Ruth *and* Beneatha *exchange amused glances.*)

Man (*regarding* Walter, *and sitting*). Well—My name is Karl Lindner . . .

Walter (*stretching out his hand*). Walter Younger. This is my wife—(Ruth *nods politely.*)—and my sister.

Lindner. How do you do.

Walter (*amiably, as he sits himself easily on a chair, leaning with interest forward on his knees and looking expectantly into the newcomer's face*). What can we do for you, Mr. Lindner!

Lindner (*some minor shuffling of the hat and briefcase on his knees*). Well—I am a representative of the Clybourne Park Improvement Association—

Walter (*pointing*). Why don't you sit your things on the floor?

Lindner. Oh—yes. Thank you. (*He slides the briefcase and hat under the chair.*) And as I was saying—I am from the Clybourne Park Improvement Association, and we have had it brought to our attention at the last meeting that you people—or at least your mother—has bought a piece of residential property at—(*He digs for the slip of paper again.*)—four o six Clybourne Street . . .

Walter. That's right. Care for something to drink? Ruth, get Mr. Lindner a beer.

Lindner (*upset for some reason*). Oh—no, really. I mean thank you very much, but no thank you.

Ruth (*innocently*). Some coffee?

Lindner. Thank you, nothing at all.

(Beneatha *is watching the man carefully.*)

Lindner. Well, I don't know how much you folks know about our organization. (*He is a gentle man, thoughtful and somewhat labored in his manner.*) It is one of these community organizations set up to look after—oh, you know, things like block upkeep and special projects, and we also have what we call our New Neighbors Orientation Committee . . .

Beneatha (*drily*). Yes—and what do they do?

Lindner (*turning a little to her and then returning the main force to* Walter). Well—it's what you might call a sort of welcoming committee, I guess. I mean they, we, I'm the chairman of the committee—go around and see the new people who move into the neighborhood and sort of give them the lowdown on the way we do things out in Clybourne Park.

Beneatha (*with appreciation of the two meanings, which escape* Ruth *and* Walter). Un-huh.

Lindner. And we also have the category of what the association calls—(*He looks elsewhere.*)—uh—special community problems . . .

Beneatha. Yes—and what are some of those?

Walter. Girl, let the man talk.

Lindner (*with understated relief*). Thank you. I would sort of like to explain this thing in my own way. I mean I want to explain to you in a certain way.

Walter. Go ahead.

Lindner. Yes. Well. I'm going to try to get right to the point. I'm sure we'll all appreciate that in the long run.

Beneatha. Yes.

Walter. Be still now!

Lindner. Well—

Ruth (*still innocently*). Would you like another chair—you don't look comfortable.

Lindner (*more frustrated than annoyed*). No, thank you very much. Please. Well—to get right to the point I—(*A great breath, and he is off at last.*) I am sure you people must be aware of some of the incidents that have happened in various parts of the city when black people have moved into certain areas—(Beneatha *exhales heavily and starts tossing a piece of fruit up and down in the air.*) Well—because we have what I think is going to be a unique type of organization in American community life—not only do we deplore that kind of thing—but we are trying to do something about it. (Beneatha *stops tossing and turns with a new and quizzical interest to the man.*) We feel—(*gaining confidence in his mission because of the interest in the faces of the people he is talking to*)—we feel that most of the trouble in this world, when you come right down to it—(*He hits his knee for emphasis.*)—most of the trouble exists because people just don't sit down and talk to each other.

Ruth (*nodding as she might in church, pleased with the remark*). You can say that again, mister.

Lindner (*more encouraged by such affirmation*). That we don't try hard enough in this world to understand the other fellow's problem. The other guy's point of view.

Ruth. Now that's right.

(Beneatha *and* Walter *merely watch and listen with genuine interest.*)

Lindner. Yes—that's the way we feel out in Clybourne Park. And that's why I was elected to come here this afternoon and talk to you people. Friendly like, you know, the way people should talk to each other and see if we couldn't find some way to work this thing out. As I say, the whole business is a matter of *caring* about the other fellow. Anybody can see that you are a nice family of folks, hard working and honest, I'm sure. (Beneatha *frowns slightly, quizzically, her head tilted regarding him.*) Today everybody knows what it means to be on the outside of *something*. And of course, there is always somebody who is out to take the advantage of people who don't always understand.

Walter. What do you mean?

Lindner. Well—you see our community is made up of people who've worked hard as the dickens for years to build up that little community. They're not rich and fancy people; just hard-working, honest people who don't really have much but those little homes and a dream of the kind of community they want to raise their children in. Now, I don't say we are perfect, and there is a lot wrong in some of the things they want. But you've got to admit that a man, right or wrong, has the right to want to have the neighborhood he lives in a certain kind of way. And at the moment the overwhelming majority of our people out there feel that people get along better, take more of a common interest in the life of the community, when they share a common background. I want you to believe me when I tell you that race prejudice simply doesn't enter into it. It is a matter of the people of Clybourne Park believing, rightly or wrongly, as I say, that for the happiness of all concerned that our Negro families are happier when they live in their *own* communities.

Beneatha (*with a grand and bitter gesture*). This, friends, is the Welcoming Committee!

Walter (*dumbfounded, looking at Lindner*). Is this what you came marching all the way over here to tell us?

Lindner. Well, now we've been having a fine conversation. I hope you'll hear me all the way through.

Walter (*tightly*). Go ahead, man.

Lindner. You see—in the face of all things I have said, we are prepared to make your family a very generous offer . . .

Beneatha. Thirty pieces and not a coin less!

Walter. Yeah?

Lindner (*putting on his glasses and drawing a form out of the briefcase*). Our association is prepared, through the collective effort of our people, to buy the house from you at a financial gain to your family.

Ruth. Lord have mercy, ain't this the living gall!

Walter. All right, you through?

Lindner. Well, I want to give you the exact terms of the financial arrangement—

Walter. We don't want to hear no exact terms of no arrangements. I want to know if you got any more to tell us 'bout getting together?

Lindner (*taking off his glasses*). Well—I don't suppose that you feel . . .

Walter. Never mind how I feel—you got any more to

say 'bout how people ought to sit down and talk to each other? . . . Get out of my house, man.

(*He turns his back and walks to the door.*)

Lindner (*looking around at the hostile faces and reaching and assembling his hat and briefcase*). Well—I don't understand why you people are reacting this way. What do you think you are going to gain by moving into a neighborhood where you just aren't wanted and where some elements—well—people can get awful worked up when they feel that their whole way of life and everything they've ever worked for is threatened.

Walter. Get out.

Lindner (*at the door, holding a small card*). Well—I'm sorry it went like this.

Walter. Get out.

Lindner (*almost sadly regarding* Walter). You just can't force people to change their hearts, son.

(*He turns and puts his card on a table and exits. Walter pushes the door to with stinging hatred and stands looking at it. Ruth just sits, and Beneatha just stands. They say nothing. Mama and Travis enter.*)

Mama. Well—this all the packing got done since I left out of here this morning? I testify before God that my children got all the energy of the dead. What time the moving men due?

Beneatha. Four o'clock. You had a caller, Mama.

(*She is smiling, teasingly.*)

Mama. Sure enough—who?

Beneatha (*her arms folded saucily*). The Welcoming Committee.

(Walter *and* Ruth *giggle.*)

Mama (*innocently*). Who?

Beneatha. The Welcoming Committee. They said they're sure going to be glad to see you when you get there.

Walter (*devilishly*). Yeah, they said they can't hardly wait to see your face.

(*laughter*)

Mama (*sensing their facetiousness*). What's the matter with you all?

Walter. Ain't nothing the matter with us. We just telling you 'bout the gentleman who came to see you this afternoon. From the Clybourne Park Improvement Association.

Mama. What he want?

Ruth (*in the same mood as* Beneatha *and* Walter). To welcome you, honey.

Walter. He said they can't hardly wait. He said the one thing they don't have, that they just *dying* to have out there, is a fine family of black people! (*to* Ruth *and* Beneatha) Ain't that right!

Ruth *and* **Beneatha** (*mockingly*). Yeah! He left his card in case—

(*They indicate the card, and* Mama *picks it up and throws it on the floor—understanding and looking off as she draws her chair up to the table on which she has put her plant and some sticks and some cord.*)

Mama. Father, give us strength. (*knowingly—and without fun*) Did he threaten us?

Beneatha. Oh—Mama—they don't do it like that any

more. He talked Brotherhood. He said everybody ought to learn how to sit down and hate each other with good Christian fellowship.

(*She and* Walter *shake hands to ridicule the remark.*)

Mama (*sadly*). Lord, protect us . . .

Ruth. You should hear the money those folks raised to buy the house from us. All we paid and then some.

Beneatha. What they think we going to do—eat 'em?

Ruth. No, honey, marry 'em.

Mama (*shaking her head*). Lord, Lord, Lord . . .

Ruth. Well—that's the way the crackers crumble. Joke.

Beneatha (*laughingly noticing what her mother is doing*). Mama, what are you doing?

Mama. Fixing my plant so it won't get hurt none on the way.

Beneatha. Mama, you going to take *that* to the new house?

Mama. Uh-huh—

Beneatha. That raggedy-looking old thing?

Mama (*stopping and looking at her*). It expresses *me*.

Ruth (*with delight, to* Beneatha). *So there*, Miss Thing!

(Walter *comes to* Mama *suddenly and bends down behind her and squeezes her in his arms with all his strength. She is overwhelmed by the suddenness of it, and though delighted, her manner is like that of* Ruth *with* Travis.)

Mama. Look out now, boy! You make me mess up my thing here!

Walter (*His face lit, he slips down on his knees beside her,* *his arms still about her.*). Mama . . . you know what it means to climb up in the chariot?

Mama (*gruffly, very happy*). Get on away from me now . . .

Ruth (*near the gift-wrapped package, trying to catch Walter's eye*). Psst—

Walter. What the old song say, Mama . . .

Ruth. Walter—Now?

(*She is pointing at the package.*)

Walter (*speaking the lines, sweetly, playfully, in his mother's face*).
*I got wings . . . you got wings . . .
All God's children got wings . . .*

Mama. Boy—get out of my face and do some work . . .

Walter.
*When I get to heaven, gonna put on my wings,
Gonna fly all over God's heaven . . .*

Beneatha (*teasingly, from across the room*). Everybody talking 'bout heaven ain't going there!

Walter (*to* Ruth, *who is carrying the box across to them*). I don't know, you think we ought to give her that? . . . Seems to me she ain't been very appreciative around here.

Mama (*eyeing the box, which is obviously a gift*). What is that?

Walter (*taking it from* Ruth *and putting it on the table in front of* Mama). Well—what you all think? Should we give it to her?

Ruth. Oh—she was pretty good today.

Mama. I'll good you—

(*She turns her eyes to the box again.*)

Beneatha. Open it, Mama.

(*She stands up, looks at it, turns and looks at all of them, and then presses her hands together and does not open the package.*)

Walter (*sweetly*). Open it, Mama. It's for you. (*Mama looks in his eyes. It is the first present in her life without its being Christmas. Slowly she opens her package and lifts out, one by one, a brand-new sparkling set of gardening tools. Walter continues, prodding.*) Ruth made up the note—read it . . .

Mama (*picking up the card and adjusting her glasses*). "To our own Mrs. Miniver—Love from Brother, Ruth, and Beneatha." Ain't that lovely . . .

Travis (*tugging at his father's sleeve*). Daddy, can I give her mine now?

Walter. All right, son. (*Travis flies to get his gift.*) Travis didn't want to go in with the rest of us, Mama. He got his own. (*somewhat amused*) We don't know what it is . . .

Travis (*racing back in the room with a large hatbox and putting it in front of his grandmother*). Here!

Mama. Lord have mercy, baby. You done gone and bought your grandmother a hat?

Travis (*very proud*). Open it!

(*She does and lifts out an elaborate, but very elaborate, wide gardening hat, and all the adults break up at the sight of it.*)

Ruth. Travis, honey, what is that?

Travis (*who thinks it is beautiful and appropriate*). It's a gardening hat! Like the ladies always have on in the magazines when they work in their gardens.

Beneatha (*giggling fiercely*). Travis—we were trying to make Mama Mrs. Miniver—not Scarlett O'Hara!

Mama (*indignantly*). What's the matter with you all! This here is a beautiful hat! (*absurdly*) I always wanted me one just like it!

(*She pops it on her head to prove it to her grandson, and the hat is ludicrous and considerably oversized.*)

Ruth. Hot dog! Go, Mama!

Walter (*doubled over with laughter*). I'm sorry, Mama— but you look like you ready to go out and chop you some cotton sure enough!

(*They all laugh except* Mama, *out of deference to* Travis's *feelings.*)

Mama (*gathering the boy up to her*). Bless your heart— this is the prettiest hat I ever owned—(Walter, Ruth, and Beneatha *chime in—noisily, festively and insincerely congratulating* Travis *on his gift.*) What are we all standing around here for? We ain't finished packin' yet. Bennie, you ain't packed one book.

(*The bell rings.*)

Beneatha. That couldn't be the movers . . . it's not hardly two good yet—

(Beneatha *goes into her room.* Mama *starts for door.*)

Walter (*turning, stiffening*). Wait—wait—I'll get it.

(*He stands and looks at the door.*)

Mama. You expecting company, son?

Walter (*just looking at the door*). Yeah—yeah . . .

(Mama *looks at* Ruth, *and they exchange innocent and unfrightened glances.*)

Mama (*not understanding*). Well, let them in, son.

Beneatha (*from her room*). We need some more string.

Mama. Travis—you run to the hardware and get me some string cord.

(Mama *goes out and* Walter *turns and looks at* Ruth. Travis *goes to a dish for money.*)

Ruth. Why don't you answer the door, man?

Walter (*suddenly bounding across the floor to her*). 'Cause sometimes it hard to let the future begin! (*stooping down in her face*)
I got wings! You got wings!
All God's children got wings!

(He *crosses to the door and throws it open. Standing there is a very slight little man in a not too prosperous business suit and with haunted frightened eyes and a hat pulled down tightly, brim up, around his forehead. Travis* passes between the men and exits. Walter *leans deep in the man's face, still in his jubilance.*)

When I get to heaven gonna put on my wings,
Gonna fly all over God's heaven . . .

(The little man just stares at him.)

Heaven—

(Suddenly he stops and looks past the little man into the empty hallway.) Where's Willy, man?

Bobo. He ain't with me.

Walter (*not disturbed*). Oh—come on in. You know my wife.

Bobo (*dumbly, taking off his hat*). Yes—h'you, Miss Ruth.

Ruth (*quietly, a mood apart from her husband already, seeing* Bobo). Hello, Bobo.

Walter. You right on time today . . . Right on time. That's the way! (*He slaps* Bobo *on his back*). Sit down . . . lemme hear.

(Ruth *stands stiffly and quietly in back of them, as though somehow she senses death, her eyes fixed on her husband.*)

Bobo (*his frightened eyes on the floor, his hat in his hands*). Could I please get a drink of water, before I tell you about it, Walter Lee?

(Walter *does not take his eyes off the man.* Ruth *goes blindly to the tap and gets a glass of water and brings it to* Bobo.)

Walter. There ain't nothing wrong, is there?

Bobo. Lemme tell you—

Walter. Man—didn't nothing go wrong?

Bobo. Lemme tell you—Walter Lee. (*looking at* Ruth *and talking to her more than to* Walter) You know how it was. I got to tell you how it was. I mean first I got to tell you how it was all the way . . . I mean about the money I put in, Walter Lee . . .

Walter (*with taut agitation now*). What about the money you put in?

Bobo. Well—it wasn't much as we told you—me and Willy—(*He stops.*) I'm sorry, Walter. I got a bad feeling about it. I got a real bad feeling about it . . .

Walter. Man, what you telling me about all this for? . . . Tell me what happened in Springfield . . .

Bobo. Springfield.

Ruth (*like a dead woman*). What was supposed to

happen in Springfield?

Bobo (*to her*). This deal that me and Walter went into with Willy—Me and Willy was going to go down to Springfield and spread some money 'round so's we wouldn't have to wait so long for the liquor license . . . That's what we were going to do. Everybody said that was the way you had to do, you understand, Miss Ruth?

Walter. Man—what happened down there?

Bobo (*a pitiful man, near tears*). I'm trying to tell you, Walter.

Walter (*screaming at him suddenly*). THEN TELL ME, DAMMIT . . . WHAT'S THE MATTER WITH YOU?

Bobo. Man . . . I didn't go to no Springfield, yesterday.

Walter (*halted, life hanging in the moment*). Why not?

Bobo (*the long way, the hard way to tell*). 'Cause I didn't have no reasons to . . .

Walter. Man, what are you talking about!

Bobo. I'm talking about the fact that when I got to the train station yesterday morning—eight o'clock like we planned . . . Man—*Willy didn't never show up.*

Walter. Why . . . where was he . . . where is he?

Bobo. That's what I'm trying to tell you . . . I don't know . . . I waited six hours . . . I called his house . . . and I waited . . . six hours . . . I waited in that train station six hours . . . (*breaking into tears*) That was all the extra money I had in the world . . . (*looking up at* Walter *with the tears running down his face*) Man, *Willy is gone.*

Walter. Gone, what you mean Willy is gone? Gone where? You mean he went by himself. You mean he went off to Springfield by himself—to take care of getting the license—(*turns and looks anxiously at* Ruth) You mean maybe he didn't want too many people in on the business down there? (*looks to* Ruth *again, as before*) You know Willy got his own ways. (*looks back to* Bobo) Maybe you was late yesterday and he just went on down there without you. Maybe—maybe—he's been callin' you at home tryin' to tell you what happened or something. Maybe—maybe—he just got sick. He's somewhere—he's got to be somewhere. We just got to find him—me and you got to find him. (*grabs* Bobo *senselessly by the collar and starts to shake him*) We got to!

Bobo (*in sudden angry, frightened agony*). What's the matter with you, Walter! *When a cat take off with your money he don't leave you no maps!*

Walter (*turning madly, as though he is looking for* Willy *in the very room*). Willy! . . . Willy . . . don't do it . . . Please don't do it . . . Man, not with that money . . . Man, please, not with that money . . . Oh, God . . . Don't let it be true . . . (*He is wandering around, crying out for* Willy *and looking for him or perhaps for help from God.*) Man . . . I trusted you . . . Man, I put my life in your hands . . . (*He starts to crumple down on the floor as* Ruth *just covers her face in horror.* Mama *opens the door and comes into the room, with* Beneatha *behind her.*) Man . . . (*He starts to pound the floor with his fists, sobbing wildly.*) *That money is made out of my father's flesh* . . .

Bobo (*standing over him helplessly*). I'm sorry, Walter . . . (*Only* Walter's *sobs reply.* Bobo *puts on his hat.*) I had my life staked on this deal, too . . .

(*He exits.*)

Mama (*to* Walter). Son—(*She goes to him, bends down to him, talks to his bent head.*) Son . . . Is it gone? Son, I gave you sixty-five hundred dollars. Is it gone? All of it? Beneatha's money too?

Walter (*lifting his head slowly*). Mama . . . I never . . . went to the bank at all . . .

Mama (*not wanting to believe him*). You mean . . . your sister's school money . . . you used that too . . . Walter? . . .

Walter Yessss! . . . All of it . . . It's all gone . . .

(*There is total silence. Ruth stands with her face covered with her hands; Beneatha leans forlornly against a wall, fingering a piece of red ribbon from the mother's gift. Mama stops and looks at her son without recognition and then, quite without thinking about it, starts to beat him senselessly in the face. Beneatha goes to them and stops it.*)

Beneatha. Mama!

(*Mama stops and looks at both of her children and rises slowly and wanders vaguely, aimlessly away from them.*)

Mama. I seen . . . him . . . night after night . . . come in . . . and look at that rug . . . and then look at me . . . the red showing in his eyes . . . the veins moving in his head . . . I seen him grow thin and old before he was forty . . . working and working and working like somebody's old horse . . . killing himself . . . and you—you give it all away in a day . . .

Beneatha. Mama—

Mama. Oh, God . . . (*She looks up to Him.*) Look down here—and show me the strength.

Beneatha. Mama—

Mama (*folding over*). Strength . . .

Beneatha (*plaintively*). Mama . . .

Mama. Strength!

THREE

An hour later.

There is a sullen light of gloom in the living room, gray light, not unlike that which began the first scene of Act One. At left we can see Walter *within his room, alone with himself. He is stretched out on the bed, his shirt out and open, his arms under his head. He does not smoke; he does not cry out; he merely lies there, looking up at the ceiling, much as if he were alone in the world.*

In the living room Beneatha *sits at the table, still surrounded by the now almost ominous packing crates. She sits looking off. We feel that this is a mood struck perhaps an hour before, and it lingers now, full of the empty sound of profound disappointment. We see on a line from her brother's bedroom the sameness of their attitudes. Presently the bell rings and* Beneatha *rises without ambition or interest in answering. It is* Asagai, *smiling broadly, striding into the room with energy and happy expectation and conversation.*

Asagai. I came over . . . I had some free time. I thought I might help with the packing. Ah, I like the look of packing crates! A household in preparation for a journey! It depresses some people . . . but for me . . . it is another feeling. Something full of the flow of life, do you understand? Movement, progress . . . It makes me think of Africa.

Beneatha. Africa!

Asagai. What kind of a mood is this? Have I told you how deeply you move me?

Beneatha. He gave away the money, Asagai . . .

Asagai. Who gave away what money?

Beneatha. The insurance money. My brother gave it away.

Asagai. Gave it away?

Beneatha. He made an investment! With a man even Travis wouldn't have trusted.

Asagai. And it's gone?

Beneatha. Gone!

Asagai. I'm very sorry . . . And you, now?

Beneatha. Me? . . . Me? . . . Me, I'm nothing . . . Me. When I was very small . . . we used to take our sleds out in the wintertime, and the only hills we had were the ice-covered stone steps of some houses down the street. And we used to fill them in with snow and make them smooth and slide down them all day . . . and it was very dangerous you know . . . far too steep . . . and sure enough one day a kid named Rufus came down too fast and hit the sidewalk . . . and we saw his face just split open right there in front of us . . . And I remember standing there looking at his bloody open face thinking that was the end of Rufus. But the ambulance came and they took him to the hospital and they fixed the broken bones and they sewed it all up . . . and the next time I saw Rufus he just had a little line down the middle of his face . . . I never got over that . . .

(Walter *sits up, listening on the bed. Throughout this scene it is important that we feel his reaction at all times, that he visibly respond to the words of his sister and* Asagai.)

Asagai. What?

Beneatha. That that was what one person could do for another, fix him up—sew up the problem, make him all right again. That was the most marvelous thing in the world . . . I wanted to do that. I always thought it was the one concrete thing in the world that a human being could do. Fix up the sick, you know—and make them whole again. This was truly being God . . .

Asagai. You wanted to be God?

Beneatha. No—I wanted to cure. It used to be so important to me. I wanted to cure. It used to matter. I used to care. I mean about people and how their bodies hurt . . .

Asagai. And you've stopped caring?

Beneatha. Yes—I think so.

Asagai. Why?

(Walter *rises, goes to the door of his room and is about to open it, then stops and stands listening, leaning on the door jamb.*)

Beneatha. Because it doesn't seem deep enough, close enough to what ails mankind—I mean this thing of sewing up bodies or administering drugs. Don't you understand? It was a child's reaction to the world. I thought that doctors had the secret to all the hurts . . . That's the way a child sees things— or an idealist.

Asagai. Children see things very well sometimes—and idealists even better.

Beneatha. I know that's what you think. Because you are still where I left off—you still care. This is what you see for the world, for Africa. You with the dreams of the future will patch up all Africa—you are going to cure the Great Sore of colonialism with Independence—

Asagai. Yes!

Beneatha. Yes—and you think that one word is the penicillin of the human spirit: "Independence!" But then what?

Asagai. That will be the problem for another time. First we must get there.

Beneatha. And where does it end?

Asagai. End? Who even spoke of an end? To life? To living?

Beneatha. An end to misery!

Asagai (*smiling*). You sound like a French intellectual.

Beneatha. No! I sound like a human being who just had her future taken right out of her hands! While I was sleeping in my bed in there, things were happening in this world that directly concerned me—and nobody asked me, consulted me—they just went out and did things—and changed my life. Don't you see there isn't any real progress, Asagai, there is only one large circle that we march in, around and around, each of us with our own little picture—in front of us—our own little mirage that we think is the future.

Asagai. That is the mistake.

Beneatha. What?

Asagai. What you just said—about the circle. It isn't a

circle—it is simply a long line—as in geometry, you know, one that reaches into infinity. And because we cannot see the end—we also cannot see how it changes. And it is very odd, but those who see the changes are called "idealists"—and those who cannot, or refuse to think, they are the "realists." It is very strange, and amusing too, I think.

Beneatha. You—you are almost religious.

Asagai. Yes . . . I think I have the religion of doing what is necessary in the world—and of worshipping man—because he is so marvelous, you see.

Beneatha. Man is foul! And the human race deserves its misery!

Asagai. You see: *you* have become the religious one in the old sense. Already, and after such a small defeat, you are worshipping despair.

Beneatha. From now on, I worship the truth—and the truth is that people are puny, small and selfish . . .

Asagai. Truth? Why is it that you despairing ones always think that only you have the truth? I never thought to see *you* like that. You! Your brother made a stupid, childish mistake—and you are grateful to him. So that now you can give up the ailing human race on account of it. You talk about what good is struggle; what good is anything? Where are we all going? And why are we bothering?

Beneatha. *And you cannot answer it!* All your talk and dreams about Africa and Independence. Independence and then what? What about all the crooks and petty thieves and just plain idiots who will come into power to steal and plunder the same as before—only now they will be black and do it in the name of the new Independence—You cannot answer that.

Asagai (*shouting over her*). *I live the answer!* (*pause*) In my village at home it is the exceptional man who can even read a newspaper . . . or who ever *sees* a book at all. I will go home, and much of what I will have to say will seem strange to the people of my village . . . But I will teach and work, and things will happen, slowly and swiftly. At times it will seem that nothing changes at all . . . and then again . . . the sudden dramatic events that make history leap into the future. And then quiet again. Retrogression even. Guns, murder, revolution. And I even will have moments when I wonder if the quiet was not better than all that death and hatred. But I will look about my village at the illiteracy and disease and ignorance, and I will not wonder long. And perhaps . . . perhaps I will be a great man . . . I mean perhaps I will hold on to the substance of truth and find my way always with the right course . . . and perhaps for it I will be butchered in my bed some night by the servants of empire . . .

Beneatha. *The martyr!*

Asagai. . . . or perhaps I shall live to be a very old man, respected and esteemed in my new nation . . . And perhaps I shall hold office, and this is what I'm trying to tell you, Alaiyo; perhaps the things I believe now for my country will be wrong and outmoded, and I will not understand and do terrible things to have things my way or merely to keep my power. Don't you see that there will be young men and women, not British soldiers then, but my own black countrymen . . . to step out of the shadows some evening and slit my then useless throat? Don't you see they have always been there . . . that they always will be? And that such a thing as my own death will be an advance? They who might kill me even . . . actually replenish me!

Beneatha. Oh, Asagai, I know all that.

Asagai. Good! Then stop moaning and groaning and tell me what you plan to do.

Beneatha. Do?

Asagai. I have a bit of a suggestion.

Beneatha. What?

Asagai (*rather quietly for him*). That when it is all over— that you come home with me—

Beneatha (*slapping herself on the forehead with exasperation born of misunderstanding*). Oh—Asagai—at this moment you decide to be romantic!

Asagai (*quickly understanding the misunderstanding*). My dear, young creature of the New World—I do not mean across the city—I mean across the ocean; home—to Africa.

Beneatha (*slowly understanding and turning to him with murmured amazement*). To—to Nigeria?

Asagai. Yes! . . . (*smiling and lifting his arms playfully*) Three hundred years later the African Prince rose up out of the seas and swept the maiden back across the middle passage over which her ancestors had come—

Beneatha (*unable to play*). Nigeria?

Asagai. Nigeria. Home. (*coming to her with genuine romantic flippancy*) I will show you our mountains and our stars, and give you cool drinks from gourds and teach you the old songs and the ways of our people—and, in time, we will pretend that— (*very softly*)—you have only been away for a day—

(*She turns her back to him, thinking. He swings her around and takes her full in his arms in a long embrace which proceeds to passion.*)

Beneatha (*pulling away*). You're getting me all mixed up—

Asagai. Why?

Beneatha. Too many things—too many things have happened today. I must sit down and think. I don't know what I feel about anything right this minute.

(*She promptly sits down and props her chin on her fist.*)

Asagai (*charmed*). All right, I shall leave you. No— don't get up. (*touching her, gently, sweetly*) Just sit awhile and think . . . Never be afraid to sit awhile and think. (*He goes to door and looks at her.*) How often I have looked at you and said, "Ah—so this is what the New World hath finally wrought . . ."

(*He exits.* Beneatha *sits on alone. Presently* Walter *enters from his room and starts to rummage through things, feverishly looking for something. She looks up and turns in her seat.*)

Beneatha (*hissingly*). Yes—just look at what the New World hath wrought! . . . Just look! (*She gestures with bitter disgust.*) There he is! *Monsieur le petit bourgeois noir*—himself! There he is—Symbol of a Rising Class! Entrepreneur! Titan of the System! (Walter *ignores her completely and continues frantically and destructively looking for something and hurling things to floor and tearing things out of their place in his search.* Beneatha *ignores the eccentricity of his actions and goes on with the monologue of insult.*) Did you dream of yachts on Lake Michigan, Brother? Did you see yourself on that Great Day sitting down at the Conference Table, surrounded by all the mighty bald-headed men in America? All halted, waiting, breathless, waiting for your pronouncements on industry? Waiting for you—Chairman of the Board? (Walter *finds what he is looking for—a small piece of white paper—and pushes it in his pocket and puts on his coat and rushes out without ever having looked at her. She shouts after him.*) I look at you and I see the final triumph of stupidity in the world!

(*The door slams, and she returns to just sitting again.* Ruth *comes quickly out of* Mama's *room.*)

Ruth. Who was that?

Beneatha. Your husband.

Ruth. Where did he go?

Beneatha. Who knows—maybe he has an appointment at U.S. Steel.

Ruth (*anxiously, with frightened eyes*). You didn't say nothing bad to him, did you?

Beneatha. Bad? Say anything bad to him? No—I told him he was a sweet boy and full of dreams and everything is strictly peachy keen, as the ofay kids say!

(Mama *enters from her bedroom. She is lost, vague, trying to catch hold, to make some sense of her former command of the world, but it still eludes her. A sense of waste overwhelms her gait; a measure of apology rides on her shoulders. She goes to her plant, which has remained on the table, looks at it, picks it up and takes it to the window sill and sets it outside, and she stands and looks at it a long moment. Then she closes the window, straightens her body with effort and turns around to her children.*)

Mama. Well—ain't it a mess in here, though? (*a false cheerfulness, a beginning of something*) I guess we all better stop moping around and get some work done. All this unpacking and everything we got to do. (Ruth *raises her head slowly in response to the sense of the line; and* Beneatha *in similar manner turns very slowly to look at her mother.*) One of you all better call the moving people and tell 'em not to come.

Ruth. Tell 'em not to come?

Mama. Of course, baby. Ain't no need in 'em coming all the way here and having to go back. They charges for that too. (*She sits down, fingers to her brow, thinking.*) Lord, ever since I was a little girl, I always remembers people saying, "Lena—Lena Eggleston, you aims too high all the time. You needs to slow down and see life a little more like it is. Just slow down some." That's what they always used to say down home—"Lord, that Lena Eggleston is a high-minded thing. She'll get her due one day!"

Ruth. No, Lena . . .

Mama. Me and Big Walter just didn't never learn right.

Ruth. Lena, no! We gotta go. Bennie—tell her . . . (*She rises and crosses to* Beneatha *with her arms outstretched.* Beneatha *doesn't respond.*) Tell her we can still move . . . the notes ain't but a hundred and twenty-five a month. We got four grown people in this house—we can work . . .

Mama (*to herself*). Just aimed too high all the time—

Ruth (*turning and going to* Mama *fast—the words pouring out with urgency and desperation*). Lena—I'll work . . . I'll work twenty hours a day in all the kitchens in

Chicago . . . I'll strap my baby on my back if I have to and scrub all the floors in America and wash all the sheets in America if I have to—but we got to move . . . We got to get out of here . . .

(Mama *reaches out absently and pats* Ruth's *hand.*)

Mama. No—I sees things differently now. Been thinking 'bout some of the things we could do to fix this place up some. I seen a second-hand bureau over on Maxwell Street just the other day that could fit right there. (*She points to where the new furniture might go.* Ruth *wanders away from her.*) Would need some new handles on it and then a little varnish and then it look like something brand-new. And—we can put up them new curtains in the kitchen . . . Why this place be looking fine. Cheer us all up so that we forget trouble ever came . . . (*to* Ruth) And you could get some nice screens to put up in your room round the baby's bassinet . . . (*She looks at both of them, pleadingly.*) Sometimes you just got to know when to give up some things . . . and hold on to what you got.

(Walter *enters from the outside, looking spent and leaning against the door, his coat hanging from him.*)

Mama. Where you been, son?

Walter (*breathing hard*). Made a call.

Mama. To who, son?

Walter. To The Man.

Mama. What man, baby?

Walter. The Man, Mama. Don't you know who The Man is?

Ruth. Walter Lee?

Walter. *The Man.* Like the guys in the streets say—The Man. Captain Boss—Mistuh Charley . . . Old Captain Please Mr. Bossman . . .

Beneatha (*suddenly*). Lindner!

Walter. That's right! That's good. I told him to come right over.

Beneatha (*fiercely, understanding*). For what? What do you want to see him for!

Walter (*looking at his sister*). We going to do business with him.

Mama. What you talking 'bout, son?

Walter. Talking 'bout life, Mama. You all always telling me to see life like it is. Well—I laid in there on my back today . . . and I figured it out. Life just like it is. Who gets and who don't get. (*He sits down with his coat on and laughs.*) Mama, you know it's all divided up. Life is. Sure enough. Between the takers and the "tooken." (*He laughs.*) I've figured it out finally. (*He looks around at them.*) Yeah. Some of us always getting "tooken." (*He laughs.*) People like Willy Harris, they don't never get "tooken." And you know why the rest of us do? 'Cause we all mixed up. Mixed up bad. We get to looking 'round for the right and the wrong; and we worry about it and cry about it and stay up nights trying to figure out 'bout the wrong and the right of things all the time . . . And all the time, man, them takers is out there operating, just taking and taking. Willy Harris? Shoot—Willy Harris don't even count. He don't even count in the big scheme of things. But I'll say one thing for old Willy Harris . . . he's taught me something. He's taught me to keep my eye on what counts in this world. Yeah—(*shouting out a little*) Thanks, Willy!

Ruth. What did you call that man for, Walter Lee?

Walter. Called him to tell him to come on over to the show. Gonna put on a show for the man. Just what he wants to see. You see, Mama, the man came here today and he told us that them people out there where you want us to move—well they so upset they willing to pay us not to move out there. (*He laughs again.*) And—and oh, Mama—you would of been proud of the way me and Ruth and Bennie acted. We told him to get out . . . Lord have mercy! We told the man to get out. Oh, we was some proud folks this afternoon, yeah. (*He lights a cigarette.*) We were still full of that old-time stuff . . .

Ruth (*coming toward him slowly*). You talking 'bout taking them people's money to keep us from moving in that house?

Walter. I ain't just talking 'bout it, baby—I'm telling you that's what's going to happen.

Beneatha. Oh, God! Where is the bottom! Where is the real honest-to-God bottom so he can't go any farther!

Walter. See—that's the old stuff. You and that boy that was here today. You all want everybody to carry a flag and a spear and sing some marching songs, huh? You wanna spend your life looking into things and trying to find the right and the wrong part, huh? Yeah. You know what's going to happen to that boy someday—he'll find himself sitting in a dungeon, locked in forever—and the takers will have the key! Forget it, baby! There ain't no causes—there ain't nothing but taking in this world, and he who takes most is smartest—and it don't make a bit of difference *how*.

Mama. You making something inside me cry, son. Some awful pain inside me.

Walter. Don't cry, Mama. Understand. That white man is going to walk in that door able to write checks for more money than we ever had. It's important to him and I'm going to help him . . . I'm going to put on the show, Mama.

Mama. Son—I come from five generations of people who was slaves and sharecroppers—but ain't nobody in my family never let nobody pay 'em no money that was a way of telling us we wasn't fit to walk the earth. We ain't never been that poor. (*raising her eyes and looking at him*) We ain't never been that dead inside.

Beneatha. Well—we are dead now. All the talk about dreams and sunlight that goes on in this house. All dead.

Walter. What's the matter with you all! I didn't make this world! It was given to me this way! Yes, I want me some yachts someday! Yes, I want to hang some real pearls 'round my wife's neck. Ain't she supposed to wear no pearls? Somebody tell me—tell me, who decides which woman is suppose to wear pearls in this world. I tell you I am a *man*—and I think my wife should wear some pearls in this world!

(*This last line hangs a good while, and* Walter *begins to move about the room. The word "Man" has penetrated his consciousness; he mumbles it to himself repeatedly between strange agitated pauses as he moves about.*)

Mama. Baby, how you going to feel on the inside?

Walter. Fine! . . . Going to feel fine . . . a man . . .

Mama. You won't have nothing left then, Walter Lee.

Walter (*coming to her*). I'm going to feel fine, Mama. I'm going to look The Man in the eyes and say— (*He falters.*)—and say, "All right, Mr. Lindner—(*He falters even more.*)—that's your neighborhood out there. You got the right to keep it like you want. You got the right to have it like you want. Just write the check and—the house is yours." And, and I am going to say—(*His voice almost breaks.*) And you—you people just put the money in my hand and you won't have to live next to this bunch of—(*He straightens up and moves away from his mother, walking around the room.*) Maybe—maybe I'll just get down on my black knees . . . (*He does so; Ruth and Bennie and Mama watch him in frozen horror.*) Captain, Mistuh, Bossman. (*He starts crying.*) A-hee-hee-hee! (*wringing his hands in profoundly anguished imitation*) Yasssssuh! Great White Father, just gi' ussen de money, fo' God's sake, and we's ain't gwine come out deh and dirty up yo' white folks neighborhood . . .

(*He breaks down completely, then gets up and goes into the bedroom.*)

Beneatha. That is not a man. That is nothing but a toothless rat.

Mama. Yes—death done come in this here house. (*She is nodding, slowly, reflectively.*) Done come walking in my house. On the lips of my children. You what supposed to be my beginning again. You—what supposed to be my harvest. (*to Beneatha*) You—you mourning your brother?

Beneatha. He's no brother of mine.

Mama. What you say?

Beneatha. I said that that individual in that room is no brother of mine.

Mama. That's what I thought you said. You feeling like you better than he is today? (Beneatha *does not answer.*) Yes? What you tell him a minute ago? That he wasn't a man? Yes? You give him up for me? You done wrote his epitaph too—like the rest of the world? Well, who give you the privilege?

Beneatha. Be on my side for once! You saw what he just did, Mama! You saw him—down on his knees. Wasn't it you who taught me—to despise any man who would do that. Do what he's going to do.

Mama. Yes—I taught you that. Me and your daddy. But I thought I taught you something else too . . . I thought I taught you to love him.

Beneatha. Love him? There is nothing left to love.

Mama. There is always something left to love. And if you ain't learned that, you ain't learned nothing. (*looking at her*) Have you cried for that boy today? I don't mean for yourself and for the family 'cause we lost the money. I mean for him; what he been through and what it done to him. Child, when do you think is the time to love somebody the most; when they done good and made things easy for everybody? Well then, you ain't through learning—because that ain't the time at all. It's when he's at his lowest and can't believe in hisself 'cause the world done whipped him so. When you starts measuring somebody, measure him right, child, measure him right. Make sure you done taken into account what hills and valleys he come through before he got to wherever he is.

(Travis *bursts into the room at the end of the speech, leaving the door open.*)

Travis. Grandmama—the moving men are downstairs!

The truck just pulled up.

Mama (*turning and looking at him*). Are they, baby? They downstairs?

(*She sighs and sits.* Lindner *appears in the doorway. He peers in and knocks lightly, to gain attention, and comes in. All turn to look at him.*)

Lindner (*hat and briefcase in hand*). Uh—hello . . .

(Ruth *crosses mechanically to the bedroom door and opens it and lets it swing open freely and slowly as the lights come up on* Walter *within, still in his coat, sitting at the far corner of the room. He looks up and out through the room to* Lindner.)

Ruth. He's here.

(*A long minute passes and* Walter *slowly gets up.*)

Lindner (*coming to the table with efficiency, putting his briefcase on the table and starting to unfold papers and unscrew fountain pens*). Well, I certainly was glad to hear from you people. (Walter *has begun the trek out of the room, slowly and awkwardly, rather like a small boy, passing the back of his sleeve across his mouth from time to time.*) Life can really be so much simpler than people let it be most of the time. Well—with whom do I negotiate? You, Mrs. Younger, or your son here? (Mama *sits with her hands folded on her lap and her eyes closed as* Walter *advances.* Travis *goes close to* Lindner *and looks at the papers curiously.*) Just some official papers, sonny.

Ruth. Travis, you go downstairs.

Mama (*opening her eyes and looking into* Walter's). No. Travis, you stay right here. And you make him understand what you doing, Walter Lee. You teach him good. Like Willy Harris taught you. You show where our five generations done come to. Go ahead, son—

Walter (*Looks down into his boy's eyes.* Travis *grins at him merrily, and* Walter *draws him beside him with his arm lightly around his shoulders*). Well, Mr. Lindner. (Beneatha *turns away.*) We called you—(*There is a profound, simple groping quality in his speech.*)—because, well, me and my family (*He looks around and shifts from one foot to the other.*) Well—we are very plain people . . .

Lindner. Yes—

Walter. I mean—I have worked as a chauffeur most of my life—and my wife here, she does domestic work in people's kitchen. So does my mother. I mean—we are plain people . . .

Lindner. Yes, Mr. Younger—

Walter (*really like a small boy, looking down at his shoes and then up at the man*). And—uh—well, my father, well, he was a laborer most of his life.

Lindner (*absolutely confused*). Uh, yes—

Walter (*looking down at his toes once again*). My father almost beat a man to death once because this man called him a bad name or something, you know what I mean?

Lindner. No, I'm afraid I don't.

Walter (*finally straightening up*). Well, what I mean is that we come from people who had a lot of pride. I mean—we are very proud people. And that's my sister over there and she's going to be a doctor—and we are very proud—

Lindner. Well—I am sure that is very nice, but—

Walter (*starting to cry and facing the man eye to eye*). What I am telling you is that we called you over here to tell you that we are very proud and that this is—this is my son, who makes the sixth generation of our family in this country, and that we have all thought about your offer and we have decided to move into our house because my father—my father—he earned it. (*Mama has her eyes closed and is rocking back and forth as though she were in church, with her head nodding the amen yes.*) We don't want to make no trouble for nobody or fight no causes—but we will try to be good neighbors. That's all we got to say. (*He looks the man absolutely in the eyes.*) We don't want your money.

(*He turns and walks away from the man.*)

Lindner (*looking around at all of them*). I take it then that you have decided to occupy.

Beneatha. That's what the man said.

Lindner (*to* Mama *in her reverie*). Then I would like to appeal to you, Mrs. Younger. You are older and wiser and understand things better I am sure . . .

Mama (*rising*). I am afraid you don't understand. My son said we was going to move and there ain't nothing left for me to say. (*shaking her head with double meaning*) You know how these young folks is nowadays, mister. Can't do a thing with 'em. Goodbye.

Lindner (*folding up his materials*). Well—if you are that final about it . . . There is nothing left for me to say. (*He finishes. He is almost ignored by the family, who are concentrating on* Walter Lee. *At the door* Lindner *halts and looks around.*) I sure hope you people know what you're doing.

(*He shakes his head and exits.*)

Ruth (*looking around and coming to life*). Well, for God's sake—if the moving men are here—LET'S GET THE HELL OUT OF HERE!

Mama (*into action*). Ain't it the truth! Look at all this here mess. Ruth, put Travis's good jacket on him . . . Walter Lee, fix your tie and tuck your shirt in; you look just like somebody's hoodlum. Lord have mercy, where is my plant? (*She flies to get it amid the general bustling of the family, who are deliberately trying to ignore the nobility of the past moment.*) You all start on down . . . Travis child, don't go empty-handed . . . Ruth, where did I put that box with my skillets in it? I want to be in charge of it myself . . . I'm going to make us the biggest dinner we ever ate tonight . . . Beneatha, what's the matter with them stockings? Pull them things up, girl . . .

(*The family starts to file out as two moving men appear and begin to carry out the heavier pieces of furniture, bumping into the family as they move about.*)

Beneatha. Mama, Asagai—asked me to marry him today and go to Africa—

Mama (*in the middle of her getting-ready activity*). He did? You ain't old enough to marry nobody—(*Seeing the moving men lifting one of her chairs precariously.*) Darling, that ain't no bale of cotton, please handle it so we can sit in it again. I had that chair twenty-five years . . .

(*The movers sigh with exasperation and go on with their work.*)

Beneatha (*girlishly and unreasonably trying to pursue the conversation*). To go to Africa, Mama—be a doctor in Africa . . .

Mama (*distracted*). Yes, baby—

Walter. Africa! What he want you to go to Africa for?

Beneatha. To practice there . . .

Walter. Girl, if you don't get all them silly ideas out your head! You better marry yourself a man with some loot . . .

Beneatha (*angrily, precisely as in the first scene of the play*). What have you got to do with who I marry!

Walter. Plenty. Now I think George Murchison—

(*He and* Beneatha *go out yelling at each other vigorously;* Beneatha *is heard saying that she would not marry George Murchison if he were Adam and she were Eve, etc. The anger is loud and real till their voices diminish.* Ruth *stands at the door and turns to* Mama *and smiles knowingly.*)

Mama (*fixing her hat at last*). Yeah—they something all right, my children . . .

Ruth. Yeah—they're something. Let's go, Lena.

Mama (*stalling, starting to look around at the house*). Yes— I'm coming. Ruth—

Ruth. Yes?

Mama (*quietly, woman to woman*). He finally come into his manhood today, didn't he? Kind of like a rainbow after the rain . . .

Ruth (*biting her lip lest her own pride explode in front of* Mama). Yes, Lena.

(Walter's *voice calls for them raucously.*)

Mama (*waving* Ruth *out vaguely*). All right, honey—go on down. I be down directly.

(Ruth *hesitates, then exits.* Mama *stands, at last alone in the living room, her plant on the table before her as the lights start to come down. She looks around at all the walls and ceilings and suddenly, despite herself, while the children call below, a great heaving thing rises in her and she puts her fist to her mouth, takes a final desperate look, pulls her coat about her, pats her hat, and goes out. The lights dim down. The door opens and she comes back in, grabs her plant, and goes out for the last time.*)

RELATED READINGS

Dreams

by Langston Hughes

*The importance of dreams was a frequent
theme in Langston Hughes's poetry.
"Harlem," the poem used in* A Raisin in
the Sun, *is about dreams that are
deferred. This poem describes what
happens when a dream dies.*

Hold fast to dreams
For if dreams die
Life is a broken-winged bird
That cannot fly.

5   Hold fast to dreams
For when dreams go
Life is a barren field
Frozen with snow.

Emerald City: Third & Pike

by Charlotte Watson Sherman

Sometimes, a dream is all a person has in life. In this story, a homeless woman tells a passerby what happened to her dreams.

This is Oya's corner. The pin-striped young executives and sleek-pumped clerk-typists, the lacquered-hair punk boys and bleached blondes with safety pins dangling from multi-holed earlobes, the frantic-eyed woman on the corner shouting obscenities, and the old-timers rambling past new high-rise fantasy hotels—all belong to Oya even though she's the only one who knows it.

Oya sits on this corner 365 days of the year, in front of the new McDonald's, with everything she needs bundled inside two plastic bags by her side. Most people pretend they don't even see Oya sitting there like a Buddha under that old green Salvation Army blanket.

Sometimes Oya's eyes look red and wild, but she won't say anything to anybody. Other times her eyes are flat, black and still as midnight outside the mission, and she talks up a furious wind.

She tells them about her family—her uncle who was a cowboy, her grandfather who fought in the Civil War, her mother who sang dirges and blues songs on the Chitlin Circuit, and her daddy who wouldn't "take no stuff from nobody," which is why they say some people got together and broke his back.

"Oh yeah, Oya be tellin them folks an earful if they'd

ever stop to listen, but she don't pay em no mind. Just keeps right on talkin, keeps right on tellin it."

One day when Oya's eyes were flat and black and she was in a preaching mood, I walked down Third & Pike, passed her as if I didn't know her. Actually I didn't. But Oya turned her eyes on me and I could feel her looking at me and I knew I couldn't just walk past this woman without saying something. So I said, "Hello."

Oya looked at me with those flat black eyes and motioned for me to take a seat by her.

Now, usually I'm afraid of folks who sit on the sidewalks downtown and look as if they've never held a job or have no place to go, but something about her eyes made me sit.

I felt foolish. I felt my face growing warm and wondered what people walking by must think of me sitting on the street next to this woman who looked as if she had nowhere to go. But after sitting there for a few minutes, it seemed as if they didn't think more or less of me than when I was walking down the street. No one paid any attention to us. That bothered me. What if I really needed help or something? What if I couldn't talk, could only sit on that street?

"Don't pay them fools no mind, daughter. They wouldn't know Moses if he walked down Pike Street and split the Nordstrom Building right down the middle. You from round here?"

I nodded my head.

"I thought so. You look like one of them folks what's been up here all they lives, kinda soft-lookin like you ain't never knowed no hard work."

I immediately took offense because I could feel the inevitable speech coming on: "There ain't no real black people in Seattle."

"Calm down, daughter, I don't mean to hurt your feelings. It's just a fact, that's all. You folks up here too cushy, too soft. Can't help it. It's the rainwater does it to you, all that water can't help but make a body soggy and spineless."

I made a move to get up.

"Now wait a minute, just wait a minute. Let me show you somethin."

She reached in her pocket and pulled out a crumpled newspaper clipping. It held a picture of a grim-faced young woman and a caption that read: "DOMESTIC TO SERVE TIME IN PRISON FOR NEAR-MURDER."

"That's me in that picture. Now ain't that somethin?"

Sure is, I thought and wondered how in the world I would get away from this woman before she hurt me.

"Them fools put me in the jail for protectin my dreams. Humph, they the only dreams I got, so naturally I'm gonna protect em. Nobody else gonna do it for me, is they?"

"But how could somebody put you in jail for protectin your dreams? That paper said you almost killed somebody."

I didn't want to seem combative but I didn't know exactly what this lady was talking about and I was feeling pretty uneasy after she'd almost insulted me then showed me evidence she'd been in jail for near-murder, no less.

"Now, I know you folks up here don't know much bout the importance of a body's dreams, but where I come from dreams was all we had. Seemed like a body got holt of a dream or a dream got holt of a body and wouldn't turn you loose. My dreams what got me through so many days of nothin, specially when it seemed like the only thing the future had to give was more of the same nothin, day after day."

She stopped abruptly and stared into space. I kept wondering what kind of dream would have forced her to try to kill somebody.

"Ain't nothin wrong with cleanin other folks' homes to make a livin. Nothin wrong with it at all. My mama had to do it and her mama had to do it at one time or nuther, so it didn't bother me none when it turned out I was gonna hafta do it too, least for a while. But my dream told me I wasn't gonna wash and scrub and shine behind other folks the rest of my life. Jobs like that was just temporary, you know what I mean?"

I nodded my head.

"Look at my hands. You never woulda knowed I danced in one of them fancy colored nightclubs and wore silk evenin gloves. Was in a sorority. Went to Xavier University."

As she reminisced, I looked at her hands. They looked rough and wide, like hands that had seen hard labor. I wondered if prison had caused them to look that way.

Oya's eyes pierced into mine. She seemed to know what I was thinking. She cackled.

"Daughter, they'd hafta put more than a prison on me to break my spirit. Don't you know it takes more than bars and beefy guards to break a fightin woman's spirit?"

She cackled some more.

"Un Un. Wouldn't never break me, and they damn sure tried. I spent fifteen years in that hellhole. Fifteen years of my precious life, all for a dreamkiller."

I looked at her and asked, "But what did you do? What did they try to do to your dreams?"

Oya leaned over to me and whispered, "I was gonna get into the space program. I was gonna be a astronaut and fly out into the universe, past all them stars. I was gonna meet up with some folks none of us never seen before, and be ambassador of goodwill; not like the fools bein sent out there now thinkin they own the universe. I was gonna be a real ambassador of goodwill and then that woman I scrubbed floors for had the nerve to tell me no black maid was ever gonna be no astronaut. Well, I could feel all the broken dreams of my mama and my grandmama and her mama swell up and start pulsin in my blood memory. I hauled off and beat that fool over the head with the mop I had in my hands till I couldn't raise up my arms no more. The chantin of my people's broken dreams died down and I looked and there was that dreamkiller in a mess of blood all over the clean floor I'd just scrubbed. And they turned round and put me in jail and never did say nothin bout that old dreamkiller. Just like my dreams never mattered. Like I didn't have no dreams. Like all I could ever think bout doin was cleanin up after nasty white folks for the rest of my life.

"Humph!" She snorted, and I almost eased to my feet so I could run if I had the cause to.

"You got any dreams, daughter?" Oya asked with a gleam in her eye.

I knew I better tell her yes, so I did.

"Well I don't care if you is from up here, you better fight for your dreams!"

Slowly, I reached out and held one of her rough hands. Then I asked, "But was your dream worth going to prison for all them years?"

Oya looked at me for a long, long time.

"I'm still gonna make it past all them stars," she said as she freed her hand and motioned for me to get to getting.

"Right now, this street b'longs to me and don't *nobody* mess with me or my dreams!" She was still shouting as I walked toward Pine Street.

The Beach Umbrella

by Cyrus Colter

Like Walter in A Raisin in the Sun, *what Elijah wants out of life is very different from what his wife wants. She's more practical than he is—"money crazy," he calls her—while his dreams are embodied in the bright colors of a beach umbrella. Whose wishes will come true?*

The Thirty-first Street beach lay dazzling under a sky so blue that Lake Michigan ran to the horizon like a sheet of sapphire silk, studded with little barbed white sequins for sails; and the heavy surface of the water lapped gently at the boulder "sea wall" which had been cut into, graded, and sanded to make the beach. Saturday afternoons were always frenzied: three black lifeguards, giants in sunglasses, preened in their towers and chaperoned the bathers—adults, teen-agers, and children—who were going through every physical gyration of which the human body is capable. Some dove, swam, some hollered, rode inner tubes, or merely stood waistdeep and pummeled the water; others—on the beach—sprinted, did handsprings and somersaults, sucked Eskimo pies, or just buried their children in the sand. Then there were the lollers—extended in their languor under a garish variety of beach umbrellas.

Elijah lolled too—on his stomach in the white sand, his chin cupped in his palm; but under no umbrella. He had none. By habit, though, he stared in awe at those who did, and sometimes meddled in their conversation: "It's gonna be gettin' *hot* pretty soon— if it ain't careful," he said to a Bantu-looking fellow and his girl sitting nearby with an older woman. The temperature was then in the nineties. The fellow managed a negligent smile. "Yeah," he said, and persisted in listening to the women. Buoyant still, Elijah watched them. But soon his gaze wavered, and then moved on to other lollers of interest. Finally he got up, stretched, brushed sand from his swimming trunks, and scanned the beach for a new spot. He started walking.

He was not tall. And he appeared to walk on his toes—his walnut-colored legs were bowed and skinny and made him hobble like a jerky little spider. Next he plopped down near two men and two girls—they were hilarious about something—sitting beneath a big purple-and-white umbrella. The girls, chocolate brown and shapely, emitted squeals of laughter at the wisecracks of the men. Elijah was enchanted. All summer long the rambunctious gaiety of the beach had fastened on him a curious charm, a hex, that brought him gawking and twiddling to the lake each Saturday. The rest of the week, save Sunday, he worked. But Myrtle, his wife, detested the sport and stayed away. Randall, the boy, had been only twice and then without little Susan, who during the summer was her mother's own midget reflection. But Elijah came regularly, especially whenever Myrtle was being evil, which he felt now was almost always. She was getting worse, too—if that was possible. The woman was money-*crazy*.

"You gotta sharp-lookin' umbrella there!" he cut in on the two laughing couples. They studied him—the abruptly silent way. Then the big-shouldered fellow smiled and lifted his eyes to their spangled roof. "Yeah? . . . Thanks," he said. Elijah carried on: "I see a lot of 'em out here this summer—much more'n last year." The fellow meditated on this, but was noncommittal. The others went on gabbing, mostly with their hands. Elijah, squinting in the hot sun, watched them. He didn't see how they could be married; they cut the fool too much, acted like they'd itched to get together for weeks and just now made it. He pondered going back in the water, but he'd already had an hour of that. His eyes traveled the sweltering beach. Funny about his folks; they were every shape and color a God-made human could be. Here was a real sample of variety—pink white to jetty black. Could you any longer call that a *race* of people? It was a complicated complication—for some real educated guy to figure out. Then another thought slowly bore in on him: the beach umbrellas blooming across the sand attracted people—slews of friends, buddies; and gals, too. Wherever the loudest-racket tore the air, a big red, or green, or yellowish umbrella—bordered with white fringe maybe—flowered in the middle of it all and gave shade to the happy good-timers.

Take, for instance, that tropical-looking pea-green umbrella over there, with the Bikini-ed brown chicks under it, and the portable radio jumping. A real beach party! He got up, stole over, and eased down in the sand at the fringe of the jubilation—two big thermos jugs sat in the shade and everybody had a paper cup in hand as the explosions of buffoonery carried out to the water. Chief provoker of mirth was a bulging-eyed old gal in a white bathing suit who, encumbered by big flabby overripe thighs, cavorted and pranced in the sand. When, perspiring from the heat, she finally fagged out, she flopped down almost on top of him. So far, he had gone unnoticed. But now, as he craned in at closer range, she brought him up: "Whatta *you* want, Pops?" She grinned, but with a touch of hostility.

Pops! Where'd she get that stuff? He was only forty-one, not a day older than that boozy bag. But he smiled. "Nothin'," he said brightly, "but you sure got one goin' here." He turned and viewed the noise-makers.

"An' you wanta get in on it!" she wrangled.

"Oh, I was just lookin'—."

"—You was just lookin'. Yeah, you was just lookin' at them young chicks there!" She roared a laugh and pointed at the sexy-looking girls under the umbrella.

Elijah grinned weakly.

"Beat it!" she catcalled, and turned back to the party.

He sat like a rock—the hell with her. But soon he relented, and wandered down to the water's edge—remote now from all inhospitality—to sit in the sand and hug his raised knees. Far out, the sailboats were pinned to the horizon and, despite all the close-in fuss, the wide miles of lake lay impassive under a blazing calm; far south and east down the long-curving lake shore, miles in the distance, the smoky haze of the Whiting plant of the Youngstown Sheet and Tube Company hung ominously in an otherwise bright sky. And so it was that he turned back and viewed the beach again—and suddenly caught his craving. Weren't they something—the umbrellas! The flashy colors of them! And the swank! No wonder folks ganged round them. Yes . . . yes, he too must have one. The thought came slow and final, and scared him. For there stood Myrtle in his mind. She nagged him now night and day, and it was always money that got her started; there was never enough—for Susan's shoes, Randy's overcoat, for new kitchen linoleum, Venetian blinds, for a better car than the old Chevy. "I just don't understand you!" she had said only night before last. "Have you got any plans at all for your family? You got a family, you know. If you could only bear to pull yourself away from that deaf old tightwad out at that warehouse, and go get yourself a *real* job. . . . But no! Not *you!*"

She was talking about old man Schroeder, who owned the warehouse where he worked. Yes, the pay could be better, but it still wasn't as bad as she made out. Myrtle could be such a fool sometimes. He had been with the old man nine years now; had started out as a freight handler, but worked up to doing inventories and a little paper work. True, the business had been going down recently, for the old man's sight and hearing were failing and his key people had left. Now he depended on *him*, Elijah—who of late wore a necktie on the job, and made his inventory rounds with a ball-point pen and clipboard. The old man was friendlier, too—almost "hat in hand" to him. He liked everything about the job now—except the pay. And that was only because of Myrtle. She just wanted so much; even talked of moving out of their rented apartment and buying out in the Chatham area. But one thing had to be said for her: she never griped about anything for herself; only for the family, the kids. Every payday he endorsed his check and handed it over to her, and got back in return only gasoline and cigarette money. And this could get pretty tiresome. About six weeks ago he'd gotten a thirty-dollar-a-month raise out of the old man, but that had only made her madder than ever. He'd thought about looking for another job all right; but where would he go to get another white-collar job? There weren't many of them for him. *She* wouldn't care if he went back to the steel mills, back to pouring that white-hot ore out at Youngstown Sheet and Tube. It would be okay with *her*—so long as his pay check was fat. But that kind of work was no good, undignified; coming home on the bus you were always so tired you went to sleep in your seat, with your lunch pail in your lap.

Just then two wet boys, chasing each other across the sand, raced by him into the water. The cold spray on his skin made him jump, jolting him out of his thoughts. He turned and slowly scanned the beach again. The umbrellas were brighter, gayer, bolder than ever—each a hiving center of playful people. He stood up finally, took a long last look, and then started back to the spot where he had parked the Chevy.

The following Monday evening was hot and humid as Elijah sat at home in their plain living room and pretended to read the newspaper; the windows were up, but not the slightest breeze came through the screens to stir Myrtle's fluffy curtains. At the moment she and nine-year-old Susan were in the kitchen finishing the dinner dishes. For twenty minutes now he had sat waiting for the furtive chance to speak to Randall. Randall, at twelve, was a serious, industrious boy, and did deliveries and odd jobs for the neighborhood grocer. Soon he came through—intent, absorbed—on his way back to the grocery store for another hour's work.

"Gotta go back, eh, Randy?" Elijah said.

"Yes, sir." He was tall for his age, and wore glasses. He paused with his hand on the doorknob.

Elijah hesitated. Better wait, he thought—wait till he comes back. But Myrtle might be around then. Better ask him now. But Randall had opened the door. "See you later, Dad," he said—and left.

Elijah, shaken, again raised the newspaper and tried to read. He should have called him back, he knew, but he had lost his nerve—because he couldn't tell how Randy would take it. Fifteen dollars was nothing though, really—Randy probably had fifty or sixty stashed away somewhere in his room. Then he thought of Myrtle, and waves of fright went over him—to be even thinking about a beach umbrella was bad enough; and to buy one, especially now, would be to her some kind of crime; but to borrow even a part of the money for it from Randy . . . well, Myrtle would go out of her mind. He had never lied to his family before. This would be the first time. And he had thought about it all day long. During the morning, at the warehouse, he had gotten out the two big mail-order catalogues, to look at the beach umbrellas; but the ones shown were all so small and dinky-looking he was contemptuous. So at noon he drove the Chevy out to a sporting-goods store on West Sixty-Third Street. There he found a gorgeous assortment of yard and beach umbrellas. And there he found his prize. A beauty, a big beauty, with wide red and white stripes, and a white fringe. But oh the price! Twenty-three dollars! And he with nine.

"What's the matter with you?" Myrtle had walked in the room. She was thin, and medium brown-skinned with a saddle of freckles across her nose, and looked harried in her sleeveless housedress with her hair unkempt.

Startled, he lowered the newspaper. "Nothing," he said.

"How can you read looking *over* the paper?"

"Was I?"

Not bothering to answer, she sank in a chair. "Susie," she called back into the kitchen, "bring my cigarettes in here, will you, baby?"

Soon Susan, chubby and solemn, with the mist of perspiration on her forehead, came in with the cigarettes. "Only three left, Mama," she said, peering into the pack.

"Okay," Myrtle sighed, taking the cigarettes. Susan started out. "Now, scour the sink good, honey—and then go take your bath. You'll feel cooler."

Before looking at him again, Myrtle lit a cigarette. "School starts in three weeks, she said, with a forlorn shake of her head. "Do you realize that?"

"Yeah? . . . Jesus, time flies." He could not look at her.

"Susie needs dresses, and a couple of pairs of *good* shoes—and she'll need a coat before it gets cold."

"Yeah, I know." He patted the arm of the chair.

"Randy—bless his heart—has already made enough to get most of *his* things. That boy's something; he's all business—I've never seen anything like it." She took a drag on her cigarette. "And old man Schroeder giving you a thirty-dollar raise! What was you thinkin' about? What'd you *say* to him?"

He did not answer at first. Finally he said, "Thirty dollars are thirty dollars, Myrtle. *You* know business is slow."

"*I'll* say it is! And there won't be any business before long—and then where'll you be? I tell you over and over again, you better start looking for something *now!* I been preachin' it to you for a year."

He said nothing.

"Ford and International Harvester are hiring every man they can lay their hands on! And the mills out in Gary and Whiting are going full blast—you see the red sky every night. The men make *good* money."

"They earn every nickel of it, too," he said in gloom.

"But they *get* it! Bring it home! It spends! Does that mean anything to you? Do you know what some of them make? Well, ask Hawthorne—or ask Sonny Milton. Sonny's wife says his checks some weeks run as high as a hundred sixty, hundred eighty, dollars. One week! Take-home pay!"

"Yeah? . . . And Sonny told me he wished he had a job like mine."

Myrtle threw back her head with a bitter gasp. "Oh-h-h, God! Did you tell him what you made? Did you tell him that?"

Suddenly Susan came back into the muggy living room. She went straight to her mother and stood as if expecting an award. Myrtle absently patted her on the side of the head. "Now, go and run your bath water, honey," she said.

Elijah smiled at Susan. "Susie," he said, "d'you know your tummy is stickin' way out—you didn't eat too much, did you?" He laughed.

Susan turned and observed him; then looked at her mother. "No," she finally said.

"Go on, now, baby," Myrtle said. Susan left the room.

Myrtle resumed. "Well, there's no use going through all this again. It's plain as the nose on your face. You got a family—a good family, *I* think. The only question is, do you wanta get off your hind end and do somethin' for it. It's just that simple."

Elijah looked at her. "You can talk real crazy sometimes, Myrtle."

"I think it's that old man!" she cried, her freckles contorted. "He's got you answering the phone, and taking inventory—wearing a necktie and all that. You wearing a necktie and your son mopping in a grocery store, so he can buy his own clothes." She snatched up her cigarettes, and walked out of the room.

His eyes did not follow her, but remained off in space. Finally he got up and went back into the kitchen. Over the stove the plaster was thinly cracked, and, in spots, the linoleum had worn through the pattern; but everything was immaculate. He opened the refrigerator, poured a glass of cold water, and sat down at the kitchen table. He felt strange and weak, and sat for a long time sipping the water.

Then after a while he heard Randall's key in the front door, sending tremors of dread through him. When Randall came into the kitchen, he seemed to him as tall as himself; his glasses were steamy from the humidity outside, and his hands were dirty.

"Hi, Dad," he said gravely without looking at him, and opened the refrigerator door.

Elijah chuckled. "Your mother'll get after you about going in there without washing your hands."

But Randall took out the water pitcher and closed the door.

Elijah watched him. Now was the time to ask him. His heart was hammering. Go on—now! But instead he heard his husky voice saying, "What'd they have you doing over at the grocery tonight?"

Randall was drinking the glass of water. When he finished he said, "Refilling shelves."

"Pretty hot job tonight, eh?"

"It wasn't so bad." Randall was matter-of-fact as he set the empty glass over the sink, and paused before leaving.

"Well . . . you're doing fine, son. Fine. Your mother sure is proud of you. . . ." Purpose had lodged in his throat.

The praise embarrassed Randall. "Okay, Dad," he said, and edged from the kitchen.

Elijah slumped back in his chair, near prostration. He tried to clear his mind of every particle of thought, but the images became only more jumbled, oppressive to the point of panic.

Then before long Myrtle came into the kitchen— ignoring him. But she seemed not so hostile now as coldly impassive, exhibiting a bravado he had not seen before. He got up and went back into the living room and turned on the television. As the TV-screen lawmen galloped before him, he sat oblivious, admitting the failure of his will. If only he could have gotten Randall to himself long enough—but everything had been so sudden, abrupt; he couldn't just ask him out of the clear blue. Besides, around him, Randall always seemed so busy, too busy to talk. He couldn't understand that; he had never mistreated the boy, never whipped him in his life; had shaken him a time or two, but that was long ago, when he was little.

He sat and watched the finish of the half-hour TV show. Myrtle was in the bedroom now. He slouched in his chair, lacking the resolve to get up and turn off the television.

Suddenly he was on his feet.

Leaving the television on, he went back to Randall's room in the rear. The door was open and Randall was asleep, lying on his back on the bed, perspiring, still dressed except for his shoes and glasses. He stood over the bed and looked at him. He was a good boy; his own son. But how strange—he thought for the first time—there was no resemblance between them. None whatsoever. Randy had a few of his mother's freckles on his thin brown face, but he could see none of himself in the boy. Then his musings were scattered by the return of his fear. He dreaded waking him. And he might be cross. If he didn't hurry, though, Myrtle or Susie might come strolling out any minute. His bones seemed rubbery from the strain. Finally he bent down and touched Randall's shoulder. The boy did not move a muscle, except to open his eyes. Elijah smiled at him. And he slowly sat up.

"Sorry, Randy—to wake you up like this."

"What's the matter?" Randall rubbed his eyes.

Elijah bent down again, but did not whisper. "Say, can you let me have fifteen bucks—till I get my check? . . . I need to get some things—and I'm a little short this time." He could hardly bring the words up.

Randall gave him a slow, queer look.

"I'll get my check a week from Friday," Elijah said, " . . . and I'll give it back to you then—sure."

Now instinctively Randall glanced toward the door, and Elijah knew Myrtle had crossed his thoughts. "You don't have to mention anything to your mother," he said with casual suddenness.

Randall got up slowly off the bed, and, in his socks, walked to the little table where he did his homework. He pulled the drawer out, fished far in the back a moment, and brought out a white business envelope secured by a rubber band. Holding the envelope close to his stomach, he took out first a ten-dollar bill, and then a five, and, sighing, handed them over.

"Thanks, old man," Elijah quivered, folding the money. "You'll get this back the day I get my check. . . . That's for sure."

"Okay," Randall finally said.

Elijah started out. Then he could see Myrtle on payday—her hand extended for his check. He hesitated, and looked at Randall, as if to speak. But he slipped the money in his trousers pocket and hurried from the room.

The following Saturday at the beach did not begin bright and sunny. By noon it was hot, but the sky was overcast and angry, the air heavy. There was no certainty whatever of a crowd, raucous or otherwise, and this was Elijah's chief concern as, shortly before twelve o'clock, he drove up in the Chevy and parked in the bumpy, graveled stretch of high ground that looked down eastward over the lake and was used for a parking lot. He climbed out of the car, glancing at the lake and clouds, and prayed in his heart it would not rain—the water was murky and restless, and only a handful of bathers had showed. But it was early yet. He stood beside the car and watched a bulbous, brown-skinned woman, in bathing suit and enormous straw hat, lugging a lunch basket down toward the beach, followed by her brood of children. And a fellow in swimming trunks, apparently the father, took a towel and sandals from his new Buick and called petulantly to his family to "just wait a minute, please." In another car, two women sat waiting, as yet fully clothed and undecided about going swimming. While down at the water's edge there was the usual cluster of dripping boys who, brash and boisterous, swarmed to the beach every day in fair weather or foul.

Elijah took off his shirt, peeled his trousers from over his swimming trunks, and started collecting the paraphernalia from the back seat of the car: a frayed pink rug filched from the house, a towel, sunglasses, cigarettes, a thermos jug filled with cold lemonade he had made himself, and a dozen paper cups. All this he stacked on the front fender. Then he went around to the rear and opened the trunk. Ah, there it lay— encased in a long, slim package trussed with heavy twine, and barely fitting athwart the spare tire. He felt prickles of excitement as he took the knife from the tool bag, cut the twine, and pulled the wrapping paper away. Red and white stripes sprang at him. It was even more gorgeous than when it had first seduced him in the store. The white fringe gave it style; the wide red fillets were cardinal and stark, and the white stripes glared. Now he opened it over his head, for the full thrill of its colors, and looked around to see if anyone else agreed. Finally after a while he gathered up all his equipment and headed down for the beach, his short, nubby legs seeming more bowed than ever under the weight of their cargo.

When he reached the sand, a choice of location became a pressing matter. That was why he had come early. From past observation it was clear that the center of gaiety shifted from day to day; last Saturday it might have been nearer the water, this Saturday, well back; or up, or down, the beach a ways. He must pick the site with care, for he could not move about the way he did when he had no umbrella; it was too noticeable. He finally took a spot as near the center of the beach as he could estimate, and dropped his gear in the sand. He knelt down and spread the pink rug, then moved the thermos jug over onto it, and folded the towel and placed it with the paper cups, sunglasses, and cigarettes down beside the jug. Now he went to find a heavy stone or brick to drive down the spike for the hollow umbrella stem to fit over. So it was not until the umbrella was finally up that he again had time for anxiety about the weather. His whole morning's effort had been an act of faith, for, as yet, there was no sun, although now and then a few azure breaks appeared in the thinning cloud mass. But before very long this brighter texture of the sky began to grow and spread by slow degrees, and his hopes quickened. Finally he sat down under the umbrella, lit a cigarette, and waited.

It was not long before two small boys came by—on their way to the water. He grinned, and called to them, "Hey, fellas, been in yet?"—their bathing suits were dry.

They stopped, and observed him. Then one of them smiled, and shook his head.

Elijah laughed. "Well, whatta you waitin' for? Go on in there and get them suits wet!" Both boys gave him silent smiles. And they lingered. He thought this a good omen—it had been different the Saturday before.

Once or twice the sun burst through the weakening clouds. He forgot the boys now in watching the skies, and soon they moved on. His anxiety was not detectable from his lazy posture under the umbrella, with his dwarfish, gnarled legs extended and his bare heels on the little rug. But then soon the clouds began to fade in earnest, seeming not to move away laterally, but slowly to recede into a lucent haze, until at last the sun came through hot and bright. He squinted at the sky and felt delivered. They would come, the folks would come!—were coming now; the beach would soon be swarming. Two other umbrellas were up already, and the diving board thronged with wet, acrobatic boys. The lifeguards were in their towers now, and still another launched his yellow rowboat. And up on the Outer Drive, the cars, one by one, were turning into the parking lot. The sun was bringing them out all right; soon he'd be in the middle of a field day. He felt a low-key, welling excitement, for the water was blue, and far out the sails were starched and white.

Soon he saw the two little boys coming back. They were soaked. Their mother—a thin, brown girl in a yellow bathing suit—was with them now, and the boys were pointing to his umbrella. She seemed dignified for her youth, as she gave him a shy glance and then smiled at the boys.

"Ah, ha!" he cried to the boys. "You've been in *now* all right!" And then laughing to her, "I was kiddin' them awhile ago about their dry bathing suits."

She smiled at the boys again. "They like for me to be with them when they go in," she said.

"I got some lemonade here," he said abruptly, slapping the thermos jug. "Why don't you have some?" His voice was anxious.

She hesitated.

He jumped up. "Come on, sit down." He smiled at her and stepped aside.

Still she hesitated. But her eager boys pressed close behind her. Finally she smiled and sat down under the umbrella.

"You fellas can sit down under there too—in the shade," he said to the boys, and pointed under the umbrella. The boys flopped down quickly in the shady sand. He started at once serving them cold lemonade in the paper cups.

"Whew! I thought it was goin' to rain there for a while," he said, making conversation after passing out the lemonade. He had squatted on the sand and lit another cigarette. "Then there wouldn't a been much goin' on. But it turned out fine after all—there'll be a mob here before long."

She sipped the lemonade, but said little. He felt she

had sat down only because of the boys, for she merely smiled and gave short answers to his questions. He learned the boys' names, Melvin and James; their ages, seven and nine; and that they were still frightened by the water. But he wanted to ask *her* name, and inquire about her husband. But he could not capture the courage.

Now the sun was hot and the sand was hot. And an orange-and-white umbrella was going up right beside them—two fellows and a girl. When the fellow who had been kneeling to drive the umbrella spike in the sand stood up, he was string-bean tall, and black, with his glistening hair freshly processed. The girl was a lighter brown, and wore a lilac bathing suit, and, although her legs were thin, she was pleasant enough to look at. The second fellow was medium, really, in height, but short beside his tall, black friend. He was yellow-skinned, and fast getting bald, although still in his early thirties. Both men sported little shoestring mustaches.

Elijah watched them in silence as long as he could. "You picked the right spot all right!" he laughed at last, putting on his sunglasses.

"How come, man?" The tall, black fellow grinned, showing his mouthful of gold teeth.

"You see *every*body here!" happily rejoined Elijah. "They all come here!"

"Man, I been coming here for years," the fellow reproved, and sat down in his khaki swimming trunks to take off his shoes. Then he stood up. "But right now, in the water I goes." He looked down at the girl. "How 'bout you, Lois, baby?"

"No, Caesar," she smiled, "not yet; I'm gonna sit here awhile and relax."

"Okay, then—you just sit right there and relax. And Little Joe"—he turned and grinned to his shorter friend—"you sit there an' relax right along with her.

You all can talk with this gentleman here"—he nodded at Elijah—"an' his nice wife." Then, pleased with himself, he trotted off toward the water.

The young mother looked at Elijah, as if he should have hastened to correct him. But somehow he had not wanted to. Yet too, Caesar's remark seemed to amuse her, for she soon smiled. Elijah felt the pain of relief— he did not want her to go; he glanced at her with a furtive laugh, and then they both laughed. The boys had finished their lemonade now, and were digging in the sand. Lois and Little Joe were busy talking.

Elijah was not quite sure what he should say to the mother. He did not understand her, was afraid of boring her, was desperate to keep her interested. As she sat looking out over the lake, he watched her. She was not pretty; and she was too thin. But he thought she had poise; he liked the way she treated her boys— tender, but casual; how different from Myrtle's frantic herding.

Soon she turned to the boys. "Want to go back in the water?" she laughed.

The boys looked at each other, and then at her. "Okay," James said finally, in resignation.

"Here, have some more lemonade," Elijah cut in.

The boys, rescued for the moment, quickly extended their cups. He poured them more lemonade, as she looked on smiling.

Now he turned to Lois and Little Joe sitting under their orange-and-white umbrella. "How 'bout some good ole cold lemonade?" he asked with a mushy smile. "I got plenty of cups." He felt he must get something going.

Lois smiled back, "No, thanks," she said, fluttering her long eyelashes, "not right now."

He looked anxiously at Little Joe.

"*I'll* take a cup!" said Little Joe, and turned and laughed to Lois: "Hand me that bag there, will you?"

He pointed to her beach bag in the sand. She passed it to him, and he reached in and pulled out a pint of gin. "We'll have some *real* lemonade," he vowed, with a daredevilish grin.

Lois squealed with pretended embarrassment. "Oh, *Joe!*"

Elijah's eyes were big now; he was thinking of the police. But he handed Little Joe a cup and poured the lemonade, to which Joe added gin. Then Joe, grinning, thrust the bottle at Elijah. "How 'bout yourself, chief?" he said.

Elijah, shaking his head, leaned forward and whispered, "You ain't supposed to drink on the beach, y'know."

"*This* ain't a drink, man—it's a taste!" said Little Joe, laughing and waving the bottle around toward the young mother. "How 'bout a little taste for your wife here?" he said to Elijah.

The mother laughed and threw up both her hands. "No, not for me!"

Little Joe gave her a rakish grin. "What'sa matter? You *'fraid* of that guy?" He jerked his thumb toward Elijah. "You 'fraid of gettin' a whippin', eh?"

"No, not exactly," she laughed.

Elijah was so elated with her his relief burst up in hysterical laughter. His laugh became strident and hoarse and he could not stop. The boys gaped at him, and then at their mother. When finally he recovered, Little Joe asked him, "Whut's so funny 'bout *that?*" Then Little Joe grinned at the mother. "You beat *him* up sometimes, eh?"

This started Elijah's hysterics all over again. The mother looked concerned now, and embarrassed; her laugh was nervous and shadowed. Little Joe glanced at Lois, laughed, and shrugged his shoulders. When Elijah finally got control of himself again he looked spent and demoralized.

Lois now tried to divert attention by starting a conversation with the boys. But the mother showed signs of restlessness and seemed ready to go. At this moment Caesar returned. Glistening beads of water ran off his long, black body; and his hair was unprocessed now. He surveyed the group and then flashed a wide, gold-toothed grin. "One big, happy family, like I said." Then he spied the paper cup in Little Joe's hand. "Whut you got there, man?"

Little Joe looked down into his cup with a playful smirk. "Lemonade, lover boy, lemonade."

"Don't hand me that jive, Joey. You ain't never had any straight lemonade in your life."

This again brought uproarious laughter from Elijah. "I got the straight lemonade *here!*" He beat the thermos jug with his hand. "Come on—have some!" He reached for a paper cup.

"Why, sure," said poised Caesar. He held out the cup and received the lemonade. "Now, gimme that gin," he said to Little Joe. Joe handed over the gin, and Caesar poured three fingers into the lemonade and sat down in the sand with his legs crossed under him. Soon he turned to the two boys, as their mother watched him with amusement. "Say, ain't you boys goin' in any more? Why don't you tell your daddy there to take you in?" He nodded toward Elijah.

Little Melvin frowned at him. "My daddy's workin'," he said.

Caesar's eyebrows shot up. "Ooooh, la, la!" he crooned. "Hey, now!" And he turned and looked at the mother and then at Elijah, and gave a clownish little snigger.

Lois tittered before feigning exasperation at him. "There you go again," she said, "talkin' when you shoulda been listening."

Elijah laughed along with the rest. But he felt deflated. Then he glanced at the mother, who was laughing too. He could detect in her no sign of dismay. Why then had she gone along with the gag in the first place, he thought—if now she didn't hate to see it punctured?

"*Hold the phone!*" softly exclaimed Little Joe. "Whut is *this?*" He was staring over his shoulder. Three women, young, brown, and worldly-looking, wandered toward them, carrying an assortment of beach paraphernalia and looking for a likely spot. They wore very scant bathing suits, and were followed, but slowly, by an older woman with big, unsightly thighs. Elijah recognized her at once. She was the old gal who, the Saturday before, had chased him away from her beach party. She wore the same white bathing suit, and one of her girls carried the pea-green umbrella.

Caesar forgot his whereabouts ogling the girls. The older woman, observing this, paused to survey the situation. "How 'bout along in here?" she finally said to one of the girls. The girl carrying the thermos jug set it in the sand so close to Caesar it nearly touched him. He was rapturous. The girl with the umbrella had no chance to put it up, for Caesar and Little Joe instantly encumbered her with help. Another girl turned on their radio, and grinning, feverish Little Joe started snapping his fingers to the music's beat.

Within a half hour, a boisterous party was in progress. The little radio, perched on a hump of sand, blared out hot jazz, as the older woman—whose name turned out to be Hattie—passed around some cold, rum-spiked punch; and before long she went into her dancing-prancing act—to the riotous delight of all, especially Elijah. Hattie did not remember him from the Saturday past, and he was glad, for everything was so different today! As different as milk and ink. He knew no one realized it, but this was *his* party really—the wildest, craziest, funniest, and best he had ever seen or heard of.

Nobody had been near the water—except Caesar, and the mother and boys much earlier. It appeared Lois was Caesar's girl friend, and she was hence more capable of reserve in face of the come-on antics of Opal, Billie, and Quanita—Hattie's girls. But Little Joe, to Caesar's tortured envy, was both free and aggressive. Even the young mother, who now volunteered her name to be Mrs. Green, got frolicsome, and twice jabbed Little Joe in the ribs.

Finally Caesar proposed they all go in the water. This met with instant, tipsy acclaim; and Little Joe, his yellow face contorted from laughing, jumped up, grabbed Billie's hand, and made off with her across the sand. But Hattie would not budge. Full of rum, and stubborn, she sat sprawled with her flaccid thighs spread in an obscene V, and her eyes half shut. Now she yelled at her departing girls: "You all watch out, now! Dont'cha go in too far. . . . Just wade! None o' you can swim a lick!"

Elijah now was beyond happiness. He felt a floating, manic glee. He sprang up and jerked Mrs. Green splashing into the water, followed by her somewhat less ecstatic boys. Caesar had to paddle about with Lois and leave Little Joe unassisted to caper with Billie, Opal, and Quanita. Billie was the prettiest of the three, and, despite Hattie's contrary statement, she could swim; and Little Joe, after taking her out in deeper water, waved back to Caesar in triumph. The sun was brazen now, and the beach and lake thronged with a variegated humanity. Elijah, a strong, but awkward, country-style swimmer, gave Mrs. Green a lesson in floating on her back, and, though she too could swim, he often felt obligated to place both his arms under her young body and buoy her up.

And sometimes he would purposely let her sink to her chin, whereupon she would feign a happy fright and utter faint simian screeches. Opal and Quanita sat in the shallows and kicked up their heels at Caesar, who, fully occupied with Lois, was a grinning water-threshing study in frustration.

Thus the party went—on and on—till nearly four o'clock. Elijah had not known the world afforded such joy; his homely face was a wet festoon of beams and smiles. He went from girl to girl, insisting she learn to float on his outstretched arms. Once begrudgingly Caesar admonished him, "Man, you gonna *drown* one o' them pretty chicks in a minute." And Little Joe bestowed his highest accolade by calling him "lover boy," as Elijah nearly strangled from laughter.

At last, they looked up to see old Hattie as she reeled down to the water's edge, coming to fetch her girls. Both Caesar and Little Joe ran out of the water to meet her, seized her by the wrists, and, despite her struggles and curses, dragged her in. "Turn me loose! You big galoots!" she yelled and gasped as the water hit her. She was in knee-deep before she wriggled and fought herself free and lurched out of the water. Her breath reeked of rum. Little Joe ran and caught her again, but she lunged backwards, and free, with such force she sat down in the wet sand with a thud. She roared a laugh now, and spread her arms for help, as her girls came sprinting and splashing out of the water and tugged her to her feet. Her eyes narrowed to vengeful, grinning slits as she turned on Caesar and Little Joe: "*I* know whut you two're up to!" She flashed a glance around toward her girls. "I been watchin' both o' you studs! Yeah, yeah, but your eyes may shine, an' your teeth may grit. . . . " She went limp in a sneering, raucous laugh. Everybody laughed now—except Lois and Mrs. Green.

They had all come out of the water now, and soon the whole group returned to their three beach umbrellas. Hattie's girls immediately prepared to break camp. They took down their pea-green umbrella, folded some wet towels, and donned their beach sandals, as Hattie still bantered Caesar and Little Joe.

"Well, you sure had *yourself* a ball today," she said to Little Joe, who was sitting in the sand.

"Comin' back next Saturday?" asked grinning Little Joe.

"I jus' might at that," surmised Hattie. "We wuz here last Saturday."

"Good! Good!" Elijah broke in. "Let's *all* come back—next Saturday!" He searched every face.

"*I'll* be here," chimed Little Joe, grinning to Caesar. Captive Caesar glanced at Lois, and said nothing.

Lois and Mrs. Green were silent. Hattie, insulted, looked at them and started swelling up. "Never mind," she said pointedly to Elijah, "You jus' come on anyhow. You'll run into a slew o' folks lookin' for a good time. You don't need no *certain* people." But a little later, she and her girls all said friendly goodbyes and walked off across the sand.

The party now took a sudden downturn. All Elijah's efforts at resuscitation seemed unavailing. The westering sun was dipping toward the distant buildings of the city, and many of the bathers were leaving. Caesar and Little Joe had become bored; and Mrs. Green's boys, whining to go, kept a reproachful eye on their mother.

"Here, you boys, take some more lemonade," Elijah said quickly, reaching for the thermos jug. "Only got a little left—better get while gettin's good!" He laughed. The boys shook their heads.

On Lois he tried cajolery. Smiling, and pointing to her wet, but trim bathing suit, he asked, "What color would you say that is?"

"Lilac," said Lois, now standing.

"It sure is pretty! Prettiest on the beach!" he whispered.

Lois gave him a weak smile. Then she reached down for her beach bag, and looked at Caesar.

Caesar stood up, "Let's cut," he turned and said to Little Joe, and began taking down their orange-and-white umbrella.

Elijah was desolate. "Whatta you goin' for? It's gettin' cooler! Now's the time to *enjoy* the beach!"

"I've got to go home," Lois said.

Mrs. Green got up now; her boys had started off already. "Just a minute, Melvin," she called, frowning. Then, smiling, she turned and thanked Elijah.

He whirled around to them all. "Are we comin' back next Saturday? Come on—let's all come back! Wasn't it great! It was *great!* Don't you think? Whatta you say?" He looked now at Lois and Mrs. Green.

"We'll see," Lois said smiling. "Maybe."

"Can *you* come?" He turned to Mrs. Green.

"I'm not sure," she said. "I'll try."

"Fine! Oh, that's fine!" He turned on Caesar and Little Joe. "I'll be lookin' for you guys, hear?"

"Okay, chief," grinned Little Joe. "An' put somethin' in that lemonade, will ya?"

Everybody laughed . . . and soon they were gone.

Elijah slowly crawled back under his umbrella, although the sun's heat was almost spent. He looked about him. There was only one umbrella on the spot now, his own; where before there had been three. Cigarette butts and paper cups lay strewn where Hattie's girls had sat, and the sandy imprint of Caesar's enormous street shoes marked his site. Mrs. Green had dropped a bobby pin. He too was caught up now by a sudden urge to go. It was hard to bear much longer—the lonesomeness. And most of the people were leaving anyway. He stirred and fidgeted in the sand, and finally started an inventory of his belongings. . . . Then his thoughts flew home, and he reconsidered. Funny—he hadn't thought of home all afternoon. Where had the time gone anyhow? . . . It seemed he'd just pulled up in the Chevy and unloaded his gear; now it was time to go home again. Then the image of solemn Randy suddenly formed in his mind, sending waves of guilt through him. He forgot where he was as the duties of his existence leapt on his back—where would he ever get Randy's fifteen dollars? He felt squarely confronted by a great blank void. It was an awful thing he had done—all for a day at the beach . . . with some sporting girls. He thought of his family and felt tiny— and him itching to come back next Saturday! Maybe Myrtle was right about him after all. Lord, if she knew what he had done. . . .

He sat there for a long time. Most of the people were gone now. The lake was quiet save for a few boys still in the water. And the sun, red like blood, had settled on the dark silhouettes of the housetops across the city. He sat beneath the umbrella just as he had at one o'clock . . . and the thought smote him. He was jolted. Then dubious. But there it was—quivering, vital, swelling inside his skull like an unwanted fetus. So this was it! He mutinied inside. So he must sell it . . . his *umbrella*. Sell it for anything—only as long as it was enough to pay back Randy. For fifteen dollars even, if necessary. He was dogged; he couldn't do it; that wasn't the answer anyway. But the thought clawed and clung to him, rebuking and coaxing him by turns, until it finally became conviction. He must do it; it was the right thing to do; the only thing to do. Maybe then the awful weight would lift, the dull commotion in his stomach cease. He got up and started collecting his belongings; placed the thermos jug, sunglasses, towel, cigarettes, and little rug together in a neat pile, to be carried to the Chevy later. Then he turned to face his umbrella. Its red and white stripes stood defiant against the wide, churned-up sand. He stood for a moment mooning at it. Then he carefully let it down and, carrying it in his right hand, went off across the sand.

The sun now had gone down behind the vast city in a shower of crimson-golden glints, and on the beach only a few stragglers remained. For his first prospects, he approached two teen-age boys, but suddenly realizing they had no money, he turned away and went over to an old woman, squat and black, in street clothes—a spectator—who stood gazing eastward out across the lake. She held in her hand a little black book, with red-edged pages, which looked like the *New Testament*. He smiled at her. "Wanna buy a nice new beach umbrella?" He held out the collapsed umbrella toward her.

She gave him a beatific smile, but shook her head. "No, son," she said, "that ain't what *I* want." And she turned to gaze out on the lake again.

For a moment he still held the umbrella out, with a question mark on his face. "Okay, then," he finally said, and went on.

Next he hurried to the water's edge, where he saw a man and two women preparing to leave. "Wanna buy a nice new beach umbrella?" His voice sounded high-pitched, as he opened the umbrella over his head. "It's brand-new. I'll sell it for fifteen dollars—it cost a lot more'n that."

The man was hostile, and glared. Finally he said, "Whatta you take me for—a fool?"

Elijah looked bewildered, and made no answer. He observed the man for a moment. Finally he let the umbrella down. As he moved away, he heard the man say to the women, "It's hot—he stole it somewhere."

Close by, another man sat alone in the sand. Elijah started toward him. The man wore trousers, but was stripped to the waist, and bent over intent on some task in his lap. When Elijah reached him, he looked up from half a hatful of cigarette butts he was breaking open for the tobacco he collected in a little paper bag. He grinned at Elijah, who meant now to pass on.

"No, I ain't interested either, buddy," the man insisted as Elijah passed him. "Not me. I jus' got *outa* jail las' week—an' ain't goin' back for no umbrella." He laughed, as Elijah kept on.

Now he saw three women, still in their bathing suits, sitting together near the diving board. They were the only people he had not yet tried—except the one lifeguard left. As he approached them, he saw that all three wore glasses and were sedate. Some schoolteachers maybe, he thought, or office workers. They were talking—until they saw him coming; then they stopped. One of them was plump, but a smooth dark brown, and sat with a towel around her shoulders. Elijah addressed them through her: "Wanna buy a nice beach umbrella?" And again he opened the umbrella over his head.

"Gee! It's beautiful," the plump woman said to the others. "But where'd you get it?" she suddenly asked Elijah, polite mistrust entering her voice.

"I bought it—just this week."

The three women looked at each other. "Why do you want to sell it so soon, then?" a second woman said.

Elijah grinned. "I need the money."

"Well!" The plump woman was exasperated. "*No,* we don't want it." And they turned from him. He stood for a while, watching them; finally he let the umbrella down and moved on.

Only the lifeguard was left. He was a huge youngster, not over twenty, and brawny and black, as he bent over cleaning out his beached rowboat. Elijah approached him so suddenly he looked up startled.

"Would you be interested in this umbrella?" Elijah said, and proffered the umbrella. "It's brand-new—I just bought it Tuesday. I'll sell it cheap." There was urgency in his voice.

The lifeguard gave him a queer stare; and then peered off toward the Outer Drive, as if looking for help. "You're lucky as hell," he finally said. "The cops just now cruised by—up on the Drive. I'd have turned you in so quick it'd made your head swim. Now you get the hell outa here." He was menacing.

Elijah was angry. "Whatta you mean? I *bought* this umbrella—it's mine."

The lifeguard took a step toward him. "I said you better get the hell outa here! An' I mean it! *You thievin' bastard, you!*"

Elijah, frightened now, gave ground. He turned and walked away a few steps; and then slowed up, as if an adequate answer had hit him. He stood for a moment. But finally he walked on, the umbrella drooping in his hand.

He walked up the gravelly slope now toward the Chevy, forgetting his little pile of belongings left in the sand. When he reached the car, and opened the trunk, he remembered; and went back down and gathered them up. He returned, threw them in the trunk and, without dressing, went around and climbed under the steering wheel. He was scared, shaken; and before starting the motor sat looking out on the lake. It was seven o'clock; the sky was waning pale, the beach forsaken, leaving a sense of perfect stillness and approaching night; the only sound was a gentle lapping of the water against the sand—one moderate *hallo-o-o-o* would have carried across to Michigan. He looked down at the beach. Where were they all now—the funny, proud, laughing people? Eating their dinners, he supposed, in a variety of homes. And all the beautiful umbrellas—where were they? Without their colors the beach was so deserted. Ah, the beach . . . after pouring hot ore all week out at the

Youngstown Sheet and Tube, he would probably be too fagged out for the beach. But maybe he wouldn't—who knew? It was great while it lasted . . . great. And his umbrella . . . he didn't know what he'd do with that . . . he might never need it again. He'd keep it, though—and see. Ha! . . . hadn't he sweat to get it! . . . and they thought he had stolen it . . . stolen it . . . ah . . . and maybe they were right. He sat for a few moments longer. Finally he started the motor, and took the old Chevy out onto the Drive in the pink-hued twilight. But down on the beach the sun was still shining.

Queens, 1963

by Julia Alvarez

*Neighborhoods rarely stay the same. In
this poem, the arrival of African-American
neighbors reminds the speaker of what it
was like when she was the outsider.*

Everyone seemed more American
than we, newly arrived,
foreign dirt still on our soles.
By year's end, a sprinkler waving
5 like a flag on our mowed lawn,
we were melted into the block,
owned our own mock Tudor house.
Then the house across the street
sold to a black family.
10 Cop cars patrolled our block
from the Castellucci's at one end
to the Balakian's on the other.
We heard rumors of bomb threats,
a burning cross on their lawn.
15 (It turned out to be a sprinkler.)
Still the neighborhood buzzed.
The barber's family, Haralambides,
our left side neighbors, didn't want trouble.
They'd come a long way to be free!
20 Mr. Scott, the retired plumber,
and his plump midwestern wife,
considered moving back home
where white and black got along
by staying where they belonged.

They had cultivated our street
like the garden she'd given up
on account of her ailing back,
bad knees, poor eyes, arthritic hands.
She went through her litany daily.
30 Politely, my mother listened—
¡Ay, Mrs. Scott, qué pena!
—her Dominican good manners
still running on automatic.
The Jewish counselor next door,
35 had a practice in her house;
clients hurried up her walk
ashamed to be seen needing.
(I watched from my upstairs window,
gloomy with adolescence,
40 and guessed how they too must have
hypocritical old world parents.)
Mrs. Bernstein said it was time
the neighborhood opened up.
As the first Jew on the block,
45 she remembered the snubbing she got
a few years back from Mrs. Scott.
But real estate worried her,
our houses' plummeting value.
She shook her head as she might
50 at a client's grim disclosures.
Too bad the world works this way.
The German girl playing the piano
down the street abruptly stopped
in the middle of a note.
55 I completed the tune in my head
as I watched *their* front door open.
A dark man in a suit
with a girl about my age
walked quickly into a car.

60 My hand lifted but fell
    before I made a welcoming gesture.
    On her face I had seen a look
    from the days before we had melted
    into the United States of America.
65 It was hardness mixed with hurt.
    It was knowing she never could be
    the right kind of American.
    A police car followed their car.
    Down the street, curtains fell back.
70 Mrs. Scott swept her walk
    as if it had just been dirtied.
    Then the German piano commenced
    downward scales as if tracking
    the plummeting real estate.
75 One by one I imagined the houses
    sinking into their lawns,
    the grass grown wild and tall
    in the past tense of this continent
    before the first foreigners owned
80 any of this free country.

Everything That Rises Must Converge

by Flannery O'Connor

This story is set shortly after the abolishment of the Jim Crow laws that forced African Americans to use separate facilities from whites. While traveling on an integrated city bus, a middle-aged white son tries to stay aloof from his mother's condescending attitude toward people of color. However, events take a turn that he doesn't expect.

Her doctor had told Julian's mother that she must lose twenty pounds on account of her blood pressure, so on Wednesday nights Julian had to take her downtown on the bus for a reducing class at the Y. The reducing class was designed for working girls over fifty, who weighed from 165 to 200 pounds. His mother was one of the slimmer ones, but she said ladies did not tell their age or weight. She would not ride the buses by herself at night since they had been integrated, and because the reducing class was one of her few pleasures, necessary for her health, and *free,* she said Julian could at least put himself out to take her, considering all she did for him. Julian did not like to consider all she did for him, but every Wednesday night he braced himself and took her.

She was almost ready to go, standing before the hall mirror, putting on her hat, while he, his hands behind him, appeared pinned to the door frame, waiting like Saint Sebastian for the arrows to begin piercing him. The hat was new and had cost her seven dollars and a half. She kept saying, "Maybe I shouldn't have paid that for it. No, I shouldn't have. I'll take it off and return it tomorrow. I shouldn't have bought it."

Julian raised his eyes to heaven. "Yes, you should have bought it," he said. "Put it on and let's go." It was a hideous hat. A purple velvet flap came down on one side of it and stood up on the other; the rest of it was green and looked like a cushion with the stuffing out. He decided it was less comical than jaunty and pathetic. Everything that gave her pleasure was small and depressed him.

She lifted the hat one more time and set it down slowly on top of her head. Two wings of gray hair protruded on either side of her florid face, but her eyes, sky-blue, were as innocent and untouched by experience as they must have been when she was ten. Were it not that she was a widow who had struggled fiercely to feed and clothe and put him through school and who was supporting him still, "until he got on his feet," she might have been a little girl that he had to take to town.

"It's all right, it's all right," he said. "Let's go." He opened the door himself and started down the walk to get her going. The sky was a dying violet and the houses stood out darkly against it, bulbous liver-colored monstrosities of a uniform ugliness though no two were alike. Since this had been a fashionable neighborhood forty years ago, his mother persisted in thinking they did well to have an apartment in it. Each house had a narrow collar of dirt around it in which sat, usually, a grubby child. Julian walked with his hands in his pockets, his head down and thrust forward and his eyes glazed with the determination to make himself completely numb during the time he would be sacrificed to her pleasure.

The door closed and he turned to find the dumpy figure, surmounted by the atrocious hat, coming toward him. "Well," she said, "you only live once and paying a little more for it, I at least won't meet myself coming and going."

"Some day I'll start making money," Julian said gloomily—he knew he never would—"and you can have one of those jokes whenever you take the fit." But first they would move. He visualized a place where the nearest neighbors would be three miles away on either side.

"I think you're doing fine," she said, drawing on her gloves. "You've only been out of school a year. Rome wasn't built in a day."

She was one of the few members of the Y reducing class who arrived in hat and gloves and who had a son who had been to college. "It takes time," she said, "and the world is in such a mess. This hat looked better on me than any of the others, though when she brought it out I said, 'Take that thing back. I wouldn't have it on my head,' and she said, 'Now wait till you see it on,' and when she put it on me, I said, 'We-ull,' and she said, 'If you ask me, that hat does something for you and you do something for the hat, and besides,' she said, 'with that hat, you won't meet yourself coming and going.'"

Julian thought he could have stood his lot better if she had been selfish, if she had been an old hag who drank and screamed at him. He walked along, saturated in depression, as if in the midst of his martyrdom he had lost his faith. Catching sight of his long, hopeless, irritated face, she stopped suddenly with a grief-stricken look, and pulled back on his arm. "Wait on me," she said. "I'm going back to the house and take this thing off and tomorrow I'm going to return it. I was out of my head. I can pay the gas bill with that seven-fifty."

He caught her arm in a vicious grip. "You are not going to take it back," he said. "I like it."

"Well," she said, "I don't think I ought . . ."

"Shut up and enjoy it," he muttered, more depressed than ever.

"With the world in the mess it's in," she said, "it's a wonder we can enjoy anything. I tell you, the bottom rail is on the top."

Julian sighed.

"Of course," she said, "if you know who you are, you can go anywhere." She said this every time he took her to the reducing class. "Most of them in it are not our kind of people," she said, "but I can be gracious to anybody. I know who I am."

"They don't give a damn for your graciousness," Julian said savagely. "Knowing who you are is good for one generation only. You haven't the foggiest idea where you stand now or who you are."

She stopped and allowed her eyes to flash at him. "I most certainly do know who I am," she said, "and if you don't know who you are, I'm ashamed of you."

"Oh hell," Julian said.

"Your great-grandfather was a former governor of this state," she said. "Your grandfather was a prosperous landowner. Your grandmother was a Godhigh."

"Will you look around you," he said tensely, "and see where you are now?" and he swept his arm jerkily out to indicate the neighborhood, which the growing darkness at least made less dingy.

"You remain what you are," she said. "Your great-grandfather had a plantation and two hundred slaves."

"There are no more slaves," he said irritably.

"They were better off when they were," she said. He groaned to see that she was off on that topic. She rolled onto it every few days like a train on an open track. He knew every stop, every junction, every swamp along the way, and knew the exact point at which her conclusion would roll majestically into the station: "It's ridiculous. It's simply not realistic. They should rise, yes, but on their own side of the fence."

"Let's skip it," Julian said.

"The ones I feel sorry for," she said, "are the ones that are half white. They're tragic."

"Will you skip it?"

"Suppose we were half white. We would certainly have mixed feelings."

"I have mixed feelings now," he groaned.

"Well let's talk about something pleasant," she said. "I remember going to Grandpa's when I was a little girl. Then the house had double stairways that went up to what was really the second floor—all the cooking was done on the first. I used to like to stay down in the kitchen on account of the way the walls smelled. I would sit with my nose pressed against the plaster and take deep breaths. Actually the place belonged to the Godhighs but your grandfather Chestny paid the mortgage and saved it for them. They were in reduced circumstances," she said, "but reduced or not, they never forgot who they were."

"Doubtless that decayed mansion reminded them," Julian muttered. He never spoke of it without contempt or thought of it without longing. He had seen it once when he was a child before it had been sold. The double stairways had rotted and been torn down. Negroes were living in it. But it remained in his mind as his mother had known it. It appeared in his dreams regularly. He would stand on the wide porch, listening to the rustle of oak leaves, then wander through the high-ceilinged hall into the parlor that opened onto it and gaze at the worn rugs and faded draperies. It occurred to him that it was he, not she, who could have appreciated it. He preferred its threadbare elegance to anything he could name and it was because of it that all the neighborhoods they had lived in had been a torment to him—whereas she had hardly known the difference. She called her insensitivity "being adjustable."

"And I remember the old darky who was my nurse, Caroline. There was no better person in the world. I've always had a great respect for my colored friends," she said. "I'd do anything in the world for them and they'd . . . "

"Will you for God's sake get off that subject?" Julian said. When he got on a bus by himself, he made it a point to sit down beside a Negro, in reparation as it were for his mother's sins.

"You're mighty touchy tonight," she said. "Do you feel all right?"

"Yes I feel all right," he said. "Now lay off."

She pursed her lips. "Well, you certainly are in a vile humor," she observed. "I just won't speak to you at all."

They had reached the bus stop. There was no bus in sight and Julian, his hands still jammed in his pockets and his head thrust forward, scowled down the empty street. The frustration of having to wait on the bus as well as ride on it began to creep up his neck like a hot hand. The presence of his mother was borne in upon him as she gave a pained sigh. He looked at her bleakly. She was holding herself very erect under the preposterous hat, wearing it like a banner of her imaginary dignity. There was in him an evil urge to break her spirit. He suddenly unloosened his tie and pulled it off and put it in his pocket.

She stiffened. "Why must you look like *that* when you take me to town?" she said. "Why must you deliberately embarrass me?"

"If you'll never learn where you are," he said, "you can at least learn where I am."

"You look like a—thug," she said.

"Then I must be one," he murmured.

"I'll just go home," she said. "I will not bother you.

If you can't do a little thing like that for me . . . "

Rolling his eyes upward, he put his tie back on. "Restored to my class," he muttered. He thrust his face toward her and hissed, "True culture is in the mind, the *mind*," he said, and tapped his head, "the mind."

"It's in the heart," she said, "and in how you do things and how you do things is because of who you *are*."

"Nobody in the damn bus cares who you are."

"I care who I am," she said icily.

The lighted bus appeared on top of the next hill and as it approached, they moved out into the street to meet it. He put his hand under her elbow and hoisted her up on the creaking step. She entered with a little smile, as if she were going into a drawing room where everyone had been waiting for her. While he put in the tokens, she sat down on one of the broad front seats for three which faced the aisle. A thin woman with protruding teeth and long yellow hair was sitting on the end of it. His mother moved up beside her and left room for Julian beside herself. He sat down and looked at the floor across the aisle where a pair of thin feet in red and white canvas sandals were planted.

His mother immediately began a general conversation meant to attract anyone who felt like talking. "Can it get any hotter?" she said and removed from her purse a folding fan, black with a Japanese scene on it, which she began to flutter before her.

"I reckon it might could," the woman with the protruding teeth said, "but I know for a fact my apartment couldn't get no hotter."

"It must get the afternoon sun," his mother said. She sat forward and looked up and down the bus. It was half filled. Everybody was white. "I see we have the bus to ourselves," she said. Julian cringed.

"For a change," said the woman across the aisle, the owner of the red and white canvas sandals. "I come on one the other day and they were thick as fleas—up front and all through."

"The world is in a mess everywhere," his mother said. "I don't know how we've let it get in this fix."

"What gets my goat is all those boys from good families stealing automobile tires," the woman with the protruding teeth said. "I told my boy, I said you may not be rich but you been raised right and if I ever catch you in any such mess, they can send you on to the reformatory. Be exactly where you belong."

"Training tells," his mother said. "Is your boy in high school?"

"Ninth grade," the woman said.

"My son just finished college last year. He wants to write but he's selling typewriters until he gets started," his mother said.

The woman leaned forward and peered at Julian. He threw her such a malevolent look that she subsided against the seat. On the floor across the aisle there was an abandoned newspaper. He got up and got it and opened it out in front of him. His mother discreetly continued the conversation in a lower tone but the woman across the aisle said in a loud voice, "Well that's nice. Selling typewriters is close to writing. He can go right from one to the other."

"I tell him," his mother said, "that Rome wasn't built in a day."

Behind the newspaper Julian was withdrawing into the inner compartment of his mind where he spent most of his time. This was a kind of mental bubble in which he established himself when he could not bear to be a part of what was going on around him. From it he could see out and judge but in it he was safe from any kind of penetration from without. It was the only place where he felt free of the general idiocy of his fellows. His mother had never entered it but from it he could see her with absolute clarity.

The old lady was clever enough and he thought that if she had started from any of the right premises, more might have been expected of her. She lived according to the laws of her own fantasy world, outside of which he had never seen her set foot. The law of it was to sacrifice herself for him after she had first created the necessity to do so by making a mess of things. If he had permitted her sacrifices, it was only because her lack of foresight had made them necessary. All of her life had been a struggle to act like a Chestny without the Chestny goods, and to give him everything she thought a Chestny ought to have; but since, said she, it was fun to struggle, why complain? And when you had won, as she had won, what fun to look back on the hard times! He could not forgive her that she had enjoyed the struggle and that she thought *she* had won.

What she meant when she said she had won was that she had brought him up successfully and had sent him to college and that he had turned out so well—good looking (her teeth had gone unfilled so that his could be straightened), intelligent (he realized he was too intelligent to be a success), and with a future ahead of him (there was of course no future ahead of him). She excused his gloominess on the grounds that he was still growing up and his radical ideas on his lack of practical experience. She said he didn't yet know a thing about "life," that he hadn't even entered the real world—when already he was as disenchanted with it as a man of fifty.

The further irony of all this was that in spite of her, he had turned out so well. In spite of going to only a third-rate college, he had, on his own initiative, come out with a first-rate education; in spite of growing up dominated by a small mind, he had ended up with a large one; in spite of all her foolish views, he was free of prejudice and unafraid to face facts. Most miraculous of all, instead of being blinded by love for her as she was for him, he had cut himself emotionally free of her and could see her with complete objectivity. He was not dominated by his mother.

The bus stopped with a sudden jerk and shook him from his meditation. A woman from the back lurched forward with little steps and barely escaped falling in his newspaper as she righted herself. She got off and a large Negro got on. Julian kept his paper lowered to watch. It gave him a certain satisfaction to see injustice in daily operation. It confirmed his view that with a few exceptions there was no one worth knowing within a radius of three hundred miles. The Negro was well dressed and carried a briefcase. He looked around and then sat down on the other end of the seat where the woman with the red and white canvas sandals was sitting. He immediately unfolded a newspaper and obscured himself behind it. Julian's mother's elbow at once prodded insistently into his ribs. "Now you see why I won't ride on these buses by myself," she whispered.

The woman with the red and white canvas sandals had risen at the same time the Negro sat down and had gone further back in the bus and taken the seat of the woman who had got off. His mother leaned forward and cast her an approving look.

Julian rose, crossed the aisle, and sat down in the place of the woman with the canvas sandals. From this position, he looked serenely across at his mother. Her face had turned an angry red. He stared at her, making his eyes the eyes of a stranger. He felt his tension suddenly lift as if he had openly declared war on her.

He would have liked to get in conversation with the Negro and to talk with him about art or politics or any subject that would be above the comprehension of those around them, but the man remained entrenched behind his paper. He was either ignoring the change of seating or had never noticed it. There was no way for Julian to convey his sympathy.

His mother kept her eyes fixed reproachfully on his face. The woman with the protruding teeth was looking at him avidly as if he were a type of monster new to her.

"Do you have a light?" he asked the Negro.

Without looking away from his paper, the man reached in his pocket and handed him a packet of matches.

"Thanks," Julian said. For a moment he held the matches foolishly. A NO SMOKING sign looked down upon him from over the door. This alone would not have deterred him; he had no cigarettes. He had quit smoking some months before because he could not afford it. "Sorry," he muttered and handed back the matches. The Negro lowered the paper and gave him an annoyed look. He took the matches and raised the paper again.

His mother continued to gaze at him but she did not take advantage of his momentary discomfort. Her eyes retained their battered look. Her face seemed to be unnaturally red, as if her blood pressure had risen. Julian allowed no glimmer of sympathy to show on his face. Having got the advantage, he wanted desperately to keep it and carry it through. He would have liked to teach her a lesson that would last her a while, but there seemed no way to continue the point. The Negro refused to come out from behind his paper.

Julian folded his arms and looked stolidly before him, facing her but as if he did not see her, as if he had ceased to recognize her existence. He visualized a scene in which, the bus having reached their stop, he would remain in his seat and when she said, "Aren't you going to get off?" he would look at her as at a stranger who had rashly addressed him. The corner they got off on was usually deserted, but it was well lighted and it would not hurt her to walk by herself the four blocks to the Y. He decided to wait until the time came and then decide whether or not he would let her get off by herself. He would have to be at the Y at ten to bring her back, but he could leave her wondering if he was going to show up. There was no reason for her to think she could always depend on him.

He retired again into the high-ceilinged room sparsely settled with large pieces of antique furniture. His soul expanded momentarily but then he became aware of his mother across from him and the vision shriveled. He studied her coldly. Her feet in little pumps dangled like a child's and did not quite reach the floor. She was training on him an exaggerated look of reproach. He felt completely detached from her. At that moment he could with pleasure have slapped her as he would have slapped a particularly obnoxious child in his charge.

He began to imagine various unlikely ways by which he could teach her a lesson. He might make friends with some distinguished Negro professor or lawyer and bring him home to spend the evening. He would be entirely justified but her blood pressure would rise to 300. He could not push her to the extent of making her have a stroke, and moreover, he had never been successful at making any Negro friends. He had tried to strike up an acquaintance on the bus with some of the better types, with ones that looked like professors or ministers or lawyers. One morning he had sat down next to a distinguished-looking dark brown man who had answered his questions with a sonorous solemnity but who had turned out to be an undertaker. Another day he had sat down beside a cigar-smoking Negro with a diamond ring on his finger, but after a few stilted pleasantries, the Negro had rung the buzzer and risen, slipping two lottery tickets into Julian's hand as he climbed over him to leave.

He imagined his mother lying desperately ill and his being able to secure only a Negro doctor for her. He toyed with that idea for a few minutes and then dropped it for a momentary vision of himself participating as a sympathizer in a sit-in demonstration. This was possible but he did not linger with it. Instead, he approached the ultimate horror. He brought home a beautiful suspiciously Negroid woman. Prepare yourself, he said. There is nothing you can do about it. This is the woman I've chosen. She's intelligent, dignified, even good, and she's suffered and she hasn't thought it *fun*. Now persecute us, go ahead and persecute us. Drive her out of here, but remember, you're driving me too. His eyes were narrowed and through the indignation he had generated, he saw his mother across the aisle, purple-faced, shrunken to the dwarf-like proportions of her moral nature, sitting like a mummy beneath the ridiculous banner of her hat.

He was tilted out of his fantasy again as the bus stopped. The door opened with a sucking hiss and out of the dark a large, gaily dressed, sullen-looking colored woman got on with a little boy. The child, who might have been four, had on a short plaid suit and a Tyrolean hat with a blue feather in it. Julian hoped that he would sit down beside him and that the woman would push in beside his mother. He could think of no better arrangement.

As she waited for her tokens, the woman was surveying the seating possibilities—he hoped with the idea of sitting where she was least wanted. There was something familiar-looking about her but Julian could not place what it was. She was a giant of a woman. Her face was set not only to meet opposition but to seek it out. The downward tilt of her large lower lip was like a warning sign: DON'T TAMPER WITH ME. Her bulging figure was encased in a green crepe dress and her feet overflowed in red shoes. She had on a hideous hat. A purple velvet flap came down on one side of it and stood up on the other; the rest of it was green and looked like a cushion with the stuffing out. She carried a mammoth red pocketbook that bulged throughout as if it were stuffed with rocks.

To Julian's disappointment, the little boy climbed up on the empty seat beside his mother. His mother lumped all children, black and white, into the common category, "cute," and she thought little Negroes were on the whole cuter than little white children. She smiled at the little boy as he climbed on the seat.

Meanwhile the woman was bearing down upon the empty seat beside Julian. To his annoyance, she squeezed herself into it. He saw his mother's face change as the woman settled herself next to him and he realized with satisfaction that this was more objectionable to her than it was to him. Her face seemed almost gray and there was a look of dull recognition in her eyes, as if suddenly she had sickened at some awful confrontation. Julian saw that it was because she and the woman had, in a sense, swapped sons. Though his mother would not realize the symbolic significance of this, she would feel it. His amusement showed plainly on his face.

The woman next to him muttered something unintelligible to herself. He was conscious of a kind of bristling next to him, a muted growling like that of an angry cat. He could not see anything but the red pocketbook upright on the bulging green thighs. He visualized the woman as she had stood waiting for her tokens—the ponderous figure, rising from the red shoes upward over the solid hips, the mammoth bosom, the haughty face, to the green and purple hat.

His eyes widened.

The vision of the two hats, identical, broke upon him with the radiance of a brilliant sunrise. His face was suddenly lit with joy. He could not believe that Fate had thrust upon his mother such a lesson. He gave a loud chuckle so that she would look at him and see that he saw. She turned her eyes on him slowly. The blue in them seemed to have turned a bruised purple. For a moment he had an uncomfortable sense of her innocence, but it lasted only a second before principle rescued him. Justice entitled him to laugh. His grin hardened until it said to her as plainly as if he were saying aloud: Your punishment exactly fits your pettiness. This should teach you a permanent lesson.

Her eyes shifted to the woman. She seemed unable to bear looking at him and to find the woman preferable. He became conscious again of the bristling presence at his side. The woman was rumbling like a volcano about to become active. His mother's mouth began to twitch slightly at one corner. With a sinking heart, he saw incipient signs of recovery on her face and realized that this was going to strike her suddenly as funny and was going to be no lesson at all. She kept her eyes on the woman and an amused smile came over her face as if the woman were a monkey that had stolen her hat. The little Negro was looking up at her with large fascinated eyes. He had been trying to attract her attention for some time.

"Carver!" the woman said suddenly. "Come heah!"

When he saw that the spotlight was on him at last, Carver drew his feet up and turned himself toward Julian's mother and giggled.

"Carver!" the woman said. "You heah me? Come heah!"

Carver slid down from the seat but remained squatting with his back against the base of it, his head turned slyly around toward Julian's mother, who was smiling at him. The woman reached a hand across the aisle and snatched him to her. He righted himself and hung backwards on her knees, grinning at Julian's mother. "Isn't he cute?" Julian's mother said to the woman with the protruding teeth.

"I reckon he is," the woman said without conviction.

The Negress yanked him upright but he eased out of her grip and shot across the aisle and scrambled, giggling wildly, onto the seat beside his love.

"I think he likes me," Julian's mother said, and smiled at the woman. It was the smile she used when she was being particularly gracious to an inferior. Julian saw everything lost. The lesson had rolled off her like rain on a roof.

The woman stood up and yanked the little boy off the seat as if she were snatching him from contagion. Julian could feel the rage in her at having no weapon like his mother's smile. She gave the child a sharp slap across his leg. He howled once and then thrust his head into her stomach and kicked his feet against her shins. "Be-have," she said vehemently.

The bus stopped and the Negro who had been reading the newspaper got off. The woman moved over and set the little boy down with a thump between herself and Julian. She held him firmly by the knee. In a moment he put his hands in front of his face and peeped at Julian's mother through his fingers.

"I see yoooooooo!" she said and put her hand in front of her face and peeped at him.

The woman slapped his hand down. "Quit yo' foolishness," she said, "before I knock the living Jesus out of you!"

Julian was thankful that the next stop was theirs. He reached up and pulled the cord. The woman reached up and pulled it at the same time. Oh my God, he thought. He had the terrible intuition that when they got off the bus together, his mother would open her purse and give the little boy a nickel. The gesture would be as natural to her as breathing. The bus stopped and the woman got up and lunged to the front, dragging the child, who wished to stay on, after her. Julian and his mother got up and followed. As they neared the door, Julian tried to relieve her of her pocketbook.

"No," she murmured, "I want to give the little boy a nickel."

"No!" Julian hissed. "No!"

She smiled down at the child and opened her bag. The bus door opened and the woman picked him up by the arm and descended with him, hanging at her hip. Once in the street she set him down and shook him.

Julian's mother had to close her purse while she got down the bus step but as soon as her feet were on the ground, she opened it again and began to rummage inside. "I can't find but a penny," she whispered, "but it looks like a new one."

"Don't do it!" Julian said fiercely between his teeth. There was a streetlight on the corner and she hurried to get under it so that she could better see into her pocketbook. The woman was heading off rapidly down the street with the child still hanging backward on her hand.

"Oh little boy!" Julian's mother called and took a few quick steps and caught up with them just beyond the lamppost. "Here's a bright new penny for you," and she held out the coin, which shone bronze in the dim light.

The huge woman turned and for a moment stood, her shoulders lifted and her face frozen with frustrated rage, and stared at Julian's mother. Then all at once she seemed to explode like a piece of machinery that had been given one ounce of pressure too much. Julian saw the black fist swing out with the red pocketbook.

He shut his eyes and cringed as he heard the woman shout, "He don't take nobody's pennies!" When he opened his eyes, the woman was disappearing down the street with the little boy staring wide-eyed over her shoulder. Julian's mother was sitting on the sidewalk.

"I told you not to do that," Julian said angrily. "I told you not to do that!"

He stood over her for a minute, gritting his teeth. Her legs were stretched out in front of her and her hat was on her lap. He squatted down and looked her in the face. It was totally expressionless. "You got exactly what you deserved," he said. "Now get up."

He picked up her pocketbook and put what had fallen out back in it. He picked the hat up off her lap. The penny caught his eye on the sidewalk and he picked that up and let it drop before her eyes into the purse. Then he stood up and leaned over and held his hands out to pull her up. She remained immobile. He sighed. Rising above them on either side were black apartment buildings, marked with irregular rectangles of light. At the end of the block a man came out of a door and walked off in the opposite direction. "All right," he said, "suppose somebody happens by and wants to know why you're sitting on the sidewalk?"

She took the hand and, breathing hard, pulled heavily up on it and then stood for a moment, swaying slightly as if the spots of light in the darkness were circling around her. Her eyes, shadowed and confused, finally settled on his face. He did not try to conceal his irritation. "I hope this teaches you a lesson," he said. She leaned forward and her eyes raked his face. She seemed trying to determine his identity. Then, as if she found nothing familiar about him, she started off with a headlong movement in the wrong direction.

"Aren't you going on to the Y?" he asked.

"Home," she muttered.

"Well, are we walking?"

For answer she kept going. Julian followed along, his hands behind him. He saw no reason to let the lesson she had had go without backing it up with an explanation of its meaning. She might as well be made to understand what had happened to her. "Don't think that was just an uppity Negro woman," he said. "That was the whole colored race which will no longer take your condescending pennies. That was your black double. She can wear the same hat as you, and to be sure," he added gratuitously (because he thought it was funny), "it looked better on her than it did on you. What all this means," he said, "is that the old world is gone. The old manners are obsolete and your graciousness is not worth a damn." He thought bitterly of the house that had been lost for him. "You aren't who you think you are," he said.

She continued to plow ahead, paying no attention to him. Her hair had come undone on one side. She dropped her pocketbook and took no notice. He stooped and picked it up and handed it to her but she did not take it.

"You needn't act as if the world had come to an end," he said, "because it hasn't. From now on you've got to live in a new world and face a few realities for a change. Buck up," he said, "it won't kill you."

She was breathing fast.

"Let's wait on the bus," he said.

"Home," she said thickly.

"I hate to see you behave like this," he said. "Just like a child. I should be able to expect more of you." He decided to stop where he was and make her stop and wait for a bus. "I'm not going any farther," he said, stopping. "We're going on the bus."

She continued to go on as if she had not heard him. He took a few steps and caught her arm and stopped her. He looked into her face and caught his breath. He was looking into a face he had never seen before. "Tell Grandpa to come get me," she said.

He stared, stricken.

"Tell Caroline to come get me," she said.

Stunned, he let her go and she lurched forward again, walking as if one leg were shorter than the other. A tide of darkness seemed to be sweeping her from him. "Mother!" he cried. "Darling, sweetheart, wait!" Crumpling, she fell to the pavement. He dashed forward and fell at her side, crying, "Mamma, Mamma!" He turned her over. Her face was fiercely distorted. One eye, large and staring, moved slightly to the left as if it had become unmoored. The other remained fixed on him, raked his face again, found nothing and closed.

"Wait here, wait here!" he cried and jumped up and began to run for help toward a cluster of lights he saw in the distance ahead of him. "Help, help!" he shouted, but his voice was thin, scarcely a thread of sound. The lights drifted farther away the faster he ran and his feet moved numbly as if they carried him nowhere. The tide of darkness seemed to sweep him back to her, postponing from moment to moment his entry into the world of guilt and sorrow.

Judith's Fancy

by Audre Lorde

*In this poem, a white person building an
expensive house discovers that her
neighbor is black. How will she react?*

Half-built
your greathouse looms
between me and the sun.
Shell-smells on the morning wind.
5   You are younger than my daughter
the boy you hold is blond
the moon is new.
My sloping land brings our eyes level
"Welcome, neighbor," I begin.

10   Were we enemies in another life
or do your eyes always turn to flint
when meeting a Black woman
face to face?

Your child speaks first.
15   "I don't like you," he cries
"Are you coming to babysit me?"

Running from Racists

by Suzanne Seixas

In 1938, Lorraine Hansberry's father bought a home in an all-white neighborhood and had to fight to the Supreme Court to stay there. Hansberry's play about segregated housing first appeared in 1959. Thirty years later, in 1989, the Long family discovers that white neighborhoods can still be hostile to African Americans.

Joann Long thought it was a prank at first. At 2:45 P.M. on December 18, 1989, her son Ray Jr.—then a 14-year-old 10th-grader at Barry Goldwater High in Phoenix—came pounding on the back door, shouting, "Let us in! The skinheads are after us!" When Joann slid open the bolt, Ray and a black school mate darted past her to the front window, obviously terrified. Peering over their shoulders, Joanne saw about 30 white youths, some carrying baseball bats and many sporting the shaved scalps and paramilitary dress of neo-Nazi "skinheads," advancing on the Longs' three-bedroom stucco home in the mostly white, middle-class neighborhood of Deer Valley. The mob kept yelling, "We're gonna get you niggers!" as it searched yard to yard for the teens.

Breathlessly, Ray Jr. explained that the gang had ambushed them after he challenged one of the "skins" for making fun of a planned rally marking the Rev. Dr. Martin Luther King, Jr.'s birthday. After quickly locking the doors and closing the drapes, Joann phoned the police and then her husband Ray, a $41,900-a-year sales manager for the cellular-telecommunications equipment maker Celwave. "I drove like a bat out of hell," recalls Ray, now 45. "But by the time I got home, the skinheads had been scared off by the police sirens." Although no one was hurt, the Longs were deeply shaken.

They are not alone: bias crimes are on the rise nationwide. Klanwatch, an arm of the Southern Poverty Law Center in Montgomery, Ala., recorded 291 race-related incidents in 41 states last year, ranging from threats to arson, bombing and even murder (the count includes only crimes where bias is known to be the main motive and thus understates the problem). The total was up 20% from the year before and fully five times higher than in 1986.

Five of the 20 murders, the biggest fraction attributed to any single group, were committed by skinheads—loosely organized gangs with 3,000 members across the country that ape the style and sometimes the racist politics of Great Britain's immigrant-bashing youths of the 1970s. In Arizona, skins have been active in the state's emotional debate on whether to become the 49th state to honor King's Jan. 15 birthday with a holiday. Some skins joined an anti-King rally last January, for example, to celebrate the defeat of the proposal by Arizona's 81%-white electorate two months earlier.

For their part, the Longs found that though their son escaped from the mob, the incident left financial scars as well as emotional ones. Specifically, they were so unsettled by the harassment that they felt compelled to move last August, even though the decision left their finances in shambles. They had to spend all their $2,300 savings to buy an $88,000, three-bedroom house in another section of Deer Valley three miles from their old home. And now their

$840 monthly mortgage payment alone is 34% higher than their old $625-a-month rent.

On the emotional side, they want to repair the fragile sense of belonging that the attack shattered. The Longs have always prided themselves on being black pioneers: they were one of the first African-American families in Deer Valley, and Ray Jr., now 16, and sister Tasha, 18, were among only three dozen blacks in the 2,045-student Barry Goldwater High School. But the family had no desire to contend with racist toughs—especially since their third child, 12-year-old Reggie, is so profoundly retarded by Down's syndrome that he cannot read, write or even talk. Ray and Joann, 39, worried that Reggie might wander away from home and run into a group of violent skinheads.

The Longs now need advice on how to budget, boost savings and provide for Reggie's future. "He'll be with Joann and me all our lives," says Ray. "But what happens after we're dead?" In addition, they need to build a solid base of diversified investments so that if they cannot flee from racism entirely, they at least won't go broke along the way.

Ray Long already has much to be proud of. Born the eighth of nine children on a family farm outside Houston, he finished high school and spent four years in the Navy before enrolling at Laney College in Oakland, Calif. in 1968. When his widowed mother fell ill two years later, he headed back to Houston and got a $12,000-a-year job as a moving-company salesman. After his mother's death, Ray married Joann Rogers, a teacher's aide from Brenham, Texas. And in 1975, the couple put $1,000 down and borrowed $18,500 at 8.5% to buy a three-bedroom house in northeast Houston.

Ray held a succession of sales jobs for local firms until he was hired by Marlboro, N. J.-based Celwave for $25,000 a year in 1984. Celwave moved the Longs to Phoenix and put Ray in charge of developing accounts in the western half of the U. S. ("Not bad for a black farm boy who never finished college," he jokes.) But since Houston's housing market was already headed downhill, Ray and Joann rented out their old home rather than sell it at a loss. The strategy worked. The roughly $3,600 annual rent more than covers the $2,400 a year they pay on the mortgage, and the property has doubled in value to about $40,000.

In Phoenix, the Longs moved into Deer Valley at the suggestion of one of Ray's white co-workers. All seemed to go well. Tasha became the first black cheerleader in the local Pop Warner Football League. Ray Jr. integrated marching bands as a drummer and won a roomful of softball trophies. Best of all, Reggie entered the district's highly regarded program for the mentally handicapped.

As more blacks moved into Deer Valley, though, racial tensions surfaced at Barry Goldwater High. At least two students proclaimed themselves skinheads. And four black youths began dressing in the trademark reds and blues of the Bloods and the Crips, the ghetto-bred Los Angeles street gangs that have been spreading nationwide.

The incident involving Ray Jr. began when one of the skinheads gave Tasha a "Heil, Hitler!" salute after hearing her mention an upcoming King rally. "I was shocked," she remembers. "I knew the skinheads were at school, but we'd never had much trouble from them." Ray Jr. confronted the white youth in the schoolyard at lunch. Name-calling swiftly escalated into threats, reinforcements arrived on both sides, and finally security guards hauled the chief antagonists off to assistant principal Wayne Kindall. "I issued warnings and thought that was the end of it," Kindall says. "But later that day the police called to say Ray Jr. had been chased." Ray could identify many of his attackers, and Kindall gave one baldpated white student a two-week suspension the following day. The police subsequently took the same boy into custody briefly but then released him, saying the case was not serious enough to warrant formal charges. "He had not committed a particularly heinous crime," explains Sgt. Kevin Robinson, "and we didn't think he was a danger to himself or others."

Galvanized into action, Joann organized a group of 20 black parents that urged the school board to ban organized gangs. The board wouldn't go that far. But in May 1990, it called for a program to encourage sensitivity to minorities (7.2% of the district's 16,000 pupils are either black or Hispanic). A black social worker directs the effort, which has since sponsored five weekend retreats attended by a total of 200 students, parents and staffers.

Still, the Longs continued to feel uncomfortable at home—especially since several of Ray Jr.'s assailants lived less than a block away. "It scared the hell out of me to hear them hanging out until 2 A.M. in their backyards," admits Ray Sr. "For a while there, I wouldn't even let our kids go to the store." So as soon as their lease expired, the Longs put $4,000 down— $2,300 in savings plus $1,700 from Ray's earnings—and assumed an $84,000, 9.5% fixed-rate mortgage to buy the home they now inhabit. Moving and closing costs totaled $1,200 and Joann spent another $1,100 on bedroom furniture.

Those outlays tightened a family budget that was already stretched by $300-a-month payments on their '83 Toyota, bought used in the spring of 1990, and the $5,400 they had spent in the previous 12 months to travel to Houston and keep up the property there. And Ray will make that budget even tighter if he goes ahead with his plan to buy a second car after his current auto loan is paid off this fall. Already, he can only afford to pay about $25 a month on outstanding charge-card balances of $900, and add a scant $150 in paycheck deductions to the $4,000 in his 401(k). That $4,000, the family's only savings, is spread among stock, fixed-income and government-obligation funds.

Considering the Longs' lack of cash, it's fortunate that both Tasha and Ray Jr. have their eyes on inexpensive Glendale Community College near Phoenix, where the tuition is only $650 a year. Tasha plans to enroll this fall, and her brother will be ready to join her in 1992.

Racial tension at Goldwater, meanwhile, has mostly dropped out of sight. "I may overhear the word nigger when I pass some white kids," says Ray Jr., "but it's not directed at me." Yet his mother worries her son may be downplaying the situation. "When I organized the black parents," says Joann, "my kids told me, 'Hey, Ma, the teachers tell us you're causing trouble.' Now my son won't say anything, because he doesn't want me going up to school and raising a ruckus." But she hasn't forgotten that day in December 1989. "As long as we live in this district and pay taxes, I'll watch the schools. We've run as far as we're going to go."

What Is Africa to Me?—A Question of Identity

by Pauli Murray

Like Beneatha, Pauli Murray had the chance to go work in Africa and to explore the African roots of her identity. While she was there, she made some surprising discoveries.

Accra, Ghana
December, 1960

I came to Africa, among other reasons, to see for myself black people in their own homeland and come to grips with the pervasive myth of innate racial inferiority that stigmatizes all people of discernible African descent in the United States. Although now widely discredited, this powerful myth shaped my growing years and gave me ambivalent feelings about myself. A remote African ancestry about which I knew little, linked with a heritage of slavery and continued inferior status in America, has been the source of a hidden shame. I need to confront the vestiges of shame embedded in my identity by making an on-the-spot assessment of my African background and my relationship to it.

Since coming to Ghana I have traveled a bit in West Africa, immersed myself in its history, and observed the life of its peoples. After living and working here for almost a year, I find that my peculiar racial history has made me irrevocably an American, a product of the New World. The romantic notion of "coming back to Mother Africa to see my people" voiced by some Negro visitors from the United States cannot change this stubborn fact. America is "home" to me, however alienated or disinherited I have felt at times.

When I ask myself "What is Africa to me?" I discover that without knowledge of personal antecedents the African past exists in a great vacuum. I haven't the slightest notion who my particular African ancestors were, what region or tribe they came from, whether they were traders, fisherfolk, herdspeople, or farmers, what their customs were or what language they spoke. There is no African village to which I can make a sentimental journey. My genetic heritage over several centuries has been too diverse to preserve physical characteristics identifying me with any tribal group. Facing a vast continent of varied peoples whose appearance, language, and customs differ from my own, I am unable to conjure up some vicarious identity and can do little more than relate to the people I meet on the basis of our common humanity. More and more I am convinced that feelings of kinship grow out of shared experience.

My foreignness is evident in my physical appearance and in my bearing, betraying my American origins. As has happened throughout human history when peoples of different cultures have come together in close contact, I am the result of considerable biological intermixture as well as cultural cross-fertilization. Some anthropologists estimate that from 70 to 80 percent of all people of color in the United States are of mixed ancestry, having European, American Indian, and Oriental as well as African forebears in varied proportions. Ashley Montagu has theorized that in the American Negro, "we are developing a distinctively new ethnic type," and suggests that the physical stamina and adaptive qualities of this type are due to "hybrid vigor." In any event, many Africans (and some Europeans living in West Africa) are puzzled by the appearance of Negroes from America. They know vaguely of their "brothers who went across the sea," but their image of these "brothers" is that of black people like themselves. Unsophisticated Africans will describe a male or female Negro from the United States as "brown man," "copper man," or sometimes "American man"—seldom "black man," as they describe themselves.

Even if my tawny color did not make me stand out from the masses of black Africans, my unconscious movements reveal my origins. On my second day in Ghana, a young workman at the law school confronted me with the question, "Tell me, Madame, are you English lady or American lady?" "What do you think?" I responded. "I think you are American lady," he said. Curious, I asked him, "How do you know?" thinking that my complexion and accent had given him the clue. Instead, he replied, "I tell by your walk; American people walk different from English people." An Israeli diplomat later confirmed this observation, assuring me that he could pick out an American walking along the street from a distinctive relaxed hip movement. I have also watched a mahogany-colored young man from the United States decked out in gorgeous Nigerian robes and headdress, only to have the local Africans laugh at him as he strolled along the street. His coloring blended with his human surroundings but he could not conceal his American gait.

Understandably, people from the United States who have suffered so many indignities because of their color hope to find an acceptable identity here, but the poignant reality is that a dark skin does not automatically qualify one to fit into the African environment. I have seen a few American Negroes exerting great effort to merge with the local population of Ghana. They have worn the *Kente* (the Ghanaian national cloth, a brilliantly colored woven fabric), eaten the local "chop," and attempted to associate only with Ghanaians. In time, they have quietly discontinued the local dress and little by little returned to American-sponsored functions. They have also wound up with digestive disorders and related ailments. On the other hand, I have met a white American born and reared near the swamps of Georgia who tells me he is able to eat local food, drink local water, and fare better against health hazards than his Negro friends from the northern United States because he built up an immunity to malaria and hookworm during his Georgia youth.

Particularly because African ancestry is associated with cruel rejections in America, finding themselves aliens in Africa is a severe jolt to those who come expecting instant acceptance from their "African brothers." They are shut off from the masses of people by barriers of language and custom and feel like outsiders in a way they never felt in the United States. They must make themselves understood by resorting to pidgin English, which offends their sensibilities. They experience all the irritations of those who come from highly industrialized countries. They have a different tempo from that of the local people and discover that their humor is not the same as African humor and their spontaneous laughter serves different functions. By contrast, white and colored Americans living and working in West Africa discover their kinship, feel outsiders together, and often find themselves seeking out one another in preference to their European or African counterparts. They speak the same language—"American"—understand the same nuances of humor, react alike to local conditions, and have a similar political outlook. Both groups recognize that their common identity sets them apart from Africans and Europeans.

Traveling about the countryside, I have not only seen piercing reminders of a radical break with the African past but have also realized how subsequent distortions of this past to justify chattel slavery in the United States contributed to a legacy of shame. When I go to villages in the interior of Ghana, where the people continue to follow many of their ancient customs, I am struck by their innate dignity, their ceremonial courtesy, and their strong sense of community cooperation in building a house or road. Although they are nonliterate and have few belongings or creature comforts, they are rooted in their own land and have a strong sense of self. An African man may house his family in a mud hut, sleep on the ground, barely make a living scrabbling in parched earth, and have only one ceremonial cloth of cheap fabric. Yet when he drapes his toga about his shoulder and comes to greet a stranger, he walks with such self-assurance that I cannot help thinking how his proud bearing contrasts with the bearing of his sharecropper counterparts I have seen in rural America. I find myself pondering the great violence done to the human spirit through American slavery and its aftermath, originally in the name of "Christianizing black savages."

The contrast is even more sharply drawn when I visit a local chief seated on a raised platform in his inner courtyard, dressed in colorful robes and surrounded by his toga-clad council of village elders. An umbrella is held over his head and his linguist stands by to communicate his greetings and responses, although the chief understands and speaks fluent English. He receives visitors according to a formal ritual marked by gravity, which includes an exchange of gifts and the pouring of a libation from the visitors' gift of costly gin drop by drop upon the ground, accompanied by solemn incantations. Here again I saw the self-possession of black people whose spirits have not been crippled by generations of repression.

I saw evidence of the break with the past and the beginnings of a new and sorrowful history in the monuments to the slave trade along the West African coast. To relive these beginnings I had to stand on the shores of the South Atlantic, in the shadow of Elmina Castle, now one of Ghana's popular tourist attractions. This great slave-trading fort on the Gulf of Guinea was built originally by the Portuguese in 1481, was captured by the Dutch in 1637, and eventually fell to the English in the eighteenth century. Surrounded on three sides by water, it was accessible by a drawbridge over a moat. I had to walk across the stone courtyard inside its high walls—today used by Ghanaian police cadets for drills—and climb the narrow winding steps to the auction room in a wing facing the ocean. Here in this high-ceilinged barnlike structure, thousands of Africans captured inland and driven to the coast by other Africans were sold to European traders for the slave markets in the Americas. Watching the auction through peepholes cut in the wall were the African chiefs who were growing rich and powerful from the lucrative trade in human flesh. They concealed themselves from their victims in a small cubicle above and to the rear of the auction area so that captives who managed to escape would never know the identity of their captors.

I had to follow in my imagination the movement of the captives as I walked through the dark, muggy dungeons, tunnel-shaped rooms, and small courtyards where they were stored awaiting shipment; I retraced their footsteps as they were herded along the black passageways under the cover of night, out through a small opening in the wall, onto the rocks above the sea, and down into the waiting canoes, which transported them to slaveships anchored offshore and to an unknown destination. Projecting myself backward in time, I tried to feel the bewilderment, the anguish, and the terror of this agonizing ordeal, which marked the introduction of Africans into America.

The young Ghanaian guide who glibly recited these historic events as he led me about could not possibly know how immediate these happenings were to me or the tumultuous emotions I felt at that moment. Tropical Africans, for whom American slavery is little more than a legend (or a political weapon), would hardly understand the shock I felt listening to a local chief tell how his great-grandfather and grandfather used to catch and sell slaves and how his grandfather often wondered what happened to those he sold. I was too numbed to tell this chief that I am only two generations removed from slavery, that my own grandmother was born a slave, and that I had seen its scars on her personality.

These experiences have left me deeply shaken, perhaps as much by the casual manner in which facts of the slave trade are related without embarrassment or feeling as by the facts themselves. I have a profound new respect for those unknown African forebears who survived the horror of that ordeal, but am filled with an unexpected bitterness when I realize the extent to which many Africans themselves participated in the slave trade, drew their wealth from it, and continued to carry it on after it was outlawed by England and the United States. I am forced to realize that the cruel exploitation of human victims by the most brutal methods is not the monopoly of any one race or nation. Thus, when I hear an African leader speaking to a world audience and demanding "restitution" for the wrongs done to the African peoples, his rhetoric leaves me unmoved. I cannot help thinking how difficult it would be to apportion blame for the wrongs done to Americans of African descent. The chain of responsibility touches too many places and peoples, including the African slave traders.

I am beginning to understand that I am the product of a new history which began on African shores but which has not been shared by Africans, a history accompanied by such radical changes in a new environment that over time it produced a new identity. For me, the net gain of coming to Africa has been to reexperience imaginatively this break in continuity as well as to gain an appreciation for the peoples and cultures who remained on the African side of the historical divide. The veil of mystery has been removed and Africans are no longer faceless peoples. They have emerged as individuals who may be kind or cruel, honest or thievish, industrious or lazy, arrogant or gentle, as the case may be. And in this knowledge of real people, lingering ghosts of the past have been exorcised. I can face all the contradictions of my American background without ambivalence and return to my country with renewed determination to claim my heritage.